The Elevated SOUL

You Are More Than What You See

BY STEPHON LEARY

A wholly owned subsidiary of **TBN**

The Elevated Soul

Trilogy Christian Publishers A Wholly Owned Subsidiary of Trinity Broadcasting Network

2442 Michelle Drive Tustin, CA 92780

Manufactured in the United States of America

10 9 8 7 6 5 4 3 2 1

Library of Congress Cataloging-in-Publication Data is available.

ISBN: 978-1-63769-434-3

E-ISBN: 978-1-63769-435-0

DEDICATION

This book is dedicated to everyone who may have experienced trauma, pain, abuse, failures, and disappointment at one time or another. Perhaps you find yourself lost, confused, hopeless, and questioning just who you are and what you were created for. Maybe you find yourself questioning can you be successful in your life and fulfill your purpose beyond what you have experienced and what you see. I want to encourage and inspire you that "you are more than what you see!" God has a purpose beyond what you see, and He loves you. He desires to use your pain for a greater purpose and elevate your soul.

ACKNOWLEDGMENTS

I would like to first thank my Lord and Savior, Jesus Christ. I thank God for using me and inspiring me to write this book! I would also like to thank everyone who picks up this book to read it. My hope and prayer are that this book inspires you, challenges you, and gives you insight to elevate your soul and find your purpose in who God made you to be.

Special thanks to my adopted parents David and Lynne Johnson, and my siblings (Jacob; Scott; Billy, rest in peace; Jessica and their families). Your constant love and support have sustained me along my journey and encouraged me through the difficult stages of my life. Thanks, Pop, for being there with me and believing in me through my invention and patent process.

Special thanks to my mother, Gladys Marie Coleman, who had the courage to run in the middle of a night and give me and my siblings an opportunity to find purpose and fulfillment in our lives. Thank you for all your hard work as a single mother through all the pain and disappointments; God has been faithful. Also, Thanks to my biological siblings for your support and encouragement (Willie, Johnny, Stephanie, Wallace, Bryan, Jessie, Jacqueline, and your families).

Special thanks to David Stallman and Gayle Stallman (Rachel, Charity), who saw something in me as a young boy. Your unselfishness, love, and support will never be forgotten.

Special thanks to the late great Hall of Fame Basketball player Pistol Pete Maravich; how can I ever forget you! Thank you for giving to the Lord. I am a life that was forever changed!

Special thanks to a very dear friend in Tammy Oneal, who was a sounding board throughout this project of writing this book, and a source of strength. Thank you for all your prayers and support and, most of all, your belief in this book.

Special thanks to Charles Knobloch, my patent attorney, who believed in my invention, the Xxcelerator Training and Rehabilitation Boot, and afforded me the opportunity to gain a patent. This process, in turn, inspired and led me to write this book.

Special thanks to Liberty University and its Engineering Department/Capstone Project Students for assisting me in the process of creating a mold and sample of the Xxcelerator Training and Rehabilitation Boot.

TABLE OF CONTENTS

Table of Contents

PREFACE

The Elevated Soul, what does that really mean? Where did this title come from? I was going through a major transition and shift in my life in 2010. I had just moved back from Laredo, Texas, and parting ways as the Head Basketball Coach at Texas A & M International University. I was returning home not in my best frame of mind, and I was looking for what was next in my life. At this point, I had been a coach on the high school and college level since 1993. During my search for what was next for me, I came in contact with a longtime friend and mentor, Tony Dutt, who was an NBA agent, in fact, the same agent who once tried to help me achieve my dream of playing professional basketball. Tony has always had an interest in me joining his company and recruiting and training the players who are under contract with him, and workout potential new clients. I was at a time in my life where I was not sure what to do next, so this time, I took him up on the offer. This was the beginning of my journey to discovering a technique and concept, which led me through a process to create and invent a Training and Rehabilitation Boot I call the "Xxcelerator."

The "Xxcelerator" was created with an "elevated sole"

in the front to cause individuals to be on the ball of their feet which is primarily where our balance is, and place us in a position where we can build strength, agility, improve by jumping, and speed. This elevated position also is the primary position to focus on building the calf muscle, and isolating strength building in the quads, glutes, hamstrings, while performing certain exercises. While enduring certain training regiments, the elevated position will also improve flexibility, strengthen tendons, and ligaments and help generate force into the ground to create an explosive quicker reaction. I am excited to get this product to the market one day soon; I believe it will be beneficial to building, training, and rehabilitating individuals in order that they may perform at their maximum level. I call it the Xxcelerator because I found through training hundreds of players and athletes, not only were they performing at higher levels and getting scholarships to college, they were also showing major increases at an accelerated level. In short periods of time, my athletes and players demonstrated tremendous improvement. I went through a long, arduous, and yet exciting journey developing and patenting this product. However, I am proud to say I completed the process thanks to my dad, David A. Johnson, patent attorney Charles Knobloch, and Liberty University School of Engineering, specifically the Capstone Project

Group; I am the inventor and patent holder of Xxcelerator Training and Rehabilitation Boot Patent #US9937374B2. So this explains the idea of the Elevated Sole-Soul aspect of why I chose this title. The other aspect of this title, *The Elevated Soul,* stems from the idea that as I was studying how an elevated sole can help athletes reach maximum performance in their prospective sports. I began to wonder about an elevated soul and how it can help us live our lives at a maximum performance through Christ. I began to have thoughts on what are the methods and requirements one must endure to live life with an elevated soul. How can we as Christians elevate our souls and be all that God has called us to be? Therefore, I'm so excited to be writing this book, yet humbled that God would use me to perhaps inspire, encourage, motivate, and change your perspective.

I believe this book has many wonderful life-changing principles that will shed light on where you are in your life and how you can achieve higher levels and maximize yourself to becoming the very best you were created to be. I first came up with the idea of writing this book on the basis of my invention of the "Training and Rehabilitation Boot." However, as I was doing some research and looking through scientific studies, I realized that to gain "optimum performance" as an athlete or person in general, we need to build athletes up, help them elevate themselves, and encourage them to execute movements through running, jumping, cutting, changing directions, stepping up or moving laterally to "elevate" their heel or to be on the ball of their feet, or some say in a dorsiflexed position. The concept is very important to the process of developing a certain amount of speed and power that can be generated and would also determine the level of athlete one can become. This was an amazing discovery for me through my invention process that enlightened me. One day I had this *aha* moment and realized as an athlete trains to perform at their maximum level, so must we train to perform at our maximum level in our lives. It was as if something spoke to me that this is the same concept that happens in our life. Think with me for a second; as a person, we must rise in every aspect of our life from being down on our heel, sort of speak. In this sense, the heel represents "being down" emotionally, physically, mentally, and spiritually. It occurred to me that if we want maximum performance in our lives, we need to "lift up" and elevate our *soul*, our faith, our emotions, and our way of thinking. This was an astonishing revelation to me. Many people say, "think positive thoughts, say positive things, get your energy up so that you may dwell on the good things in your life and in the world!" This may be true; however, I have learned that most people do not know what that really means. I thought some people are born flatfooted and have fallen arches or born into a down situation and environment. Some people throughout their lives find themselves in a downward state because of what others do to them.

Often as I trained my players and athletes, I was training their character, their state of mind, and emotions, sometimes more so than I was training them physically. Being the Christian man that I am, I had an awakening that many times I was sharing the purpose God had for each of them through whatever they might be experiencing. Whether it was how they were being treated by their school coach, teammate, mom, dad, siblings, and friends, I was speaking life into them to elevate their *soul*. Many times, I could tell them what to do physically, but it did not help because they were down in their spirit. In my programs, I would always share what I called a *nugget*, a quick five minutes of wisdom often from the Bible or a good book to open practices, and even before games. I also realized that the good ole coach speak wasn't getting through, quotes like "you can do it," "if you fall, get up," "failure is not an option," "don't you dare quit," "keep fighting," "believe in yourself," "don't let them break you," all these things are good to say, but when we are going through a downtime or flatfooted time in our life there is nothing, absolutely nothing, that can substitute a good touch from

God, where His spirit penetrates the heart and soul of deep despair. Furthermore, life sometimes happens, and we need something far greater than ourselves to get us through, to pick us up, and to help us find the strength to continue this journey in our lives. That something for me was my relationship with God, and I believe it is for you. I have found myself flatfooted or down on my luck in life, and the only thing or person that could help me is my Lord and Savior, Jesus Christ. Scripture tells us, "I will lift up mine eyes unto the hills, from whence cometh my help. My help comes from the Lord which maketh Heaven and Earth" (Psalm121:1-2, KJV).

After all, footwork forms the foundation of almost all sports. In football, track, soccer, and other running sports, your feet are the springs and levers that cushion and propel you to perform at your maximum potential. In basketball and volleyball, your feet are your launching pads for your leaps, jumps, and elevation. In tennis and aerobics, they act as brakes and pivots for side-to-side motions. They are formidable weapons in martial arts, dainty pillars in ballet, and grippers and levers for climbing. By their unique structure, your feet simultaneously support your weight, balance and propel you, and safely absorb the shocks of your motion. In fact, sprinters run on the balls of their feet and finish the stride by driving through the toes. How compelling is it to know that God is our feet and foundation, where our soul is elevated to live and perform our best in this life? It is through His feet and our feet we walk through life built on His foundation. God compares making our feet like a deer throughout the Scriptures. This is *so* amazing and fascinating because the deer is described as an animal with an elevated sole. The deer does not have a heel to sit back on. It is always in position, act and move with speed and cut with precision, and jump high. Isn't it ironic I am sharing with you how you can elevate your soul, like the position of the deer? Check out these Scriptures: 2 Samuel 22:32-35 (NIV).

> **For who is God besides the Lord? And who is the Rock except our God? It is God who arms me with strength and keeps my way secure. He makes my feet like the feet of a deer; He causes me to stand on the heights. He trains my hands for battle; my arms can bend a bow of bronze.**

> **He makes my feet like hinds' feet and sets me upon my high places. He trains my hands for battle, so that my arms can bend a bow of bronze. You have also given me the shield of Your salvation, And Your right hand upholds me; And Your gentleness makes me great. You enlarge my steps under me, and my**

feet have not slipped.

Psalm 18:33-36 (NASB)

Amazing Scripture, absolutely amazing! God is ready to elevate you and set you in high places. He wants to train you so that you are armed for the battle of life. Through my inventing and creating the "Training and Rehabilitation Boot," I learned the true meaning of an elevated soul in my life—it has changed my life and perspective. So, this is why I titled this book *The Elevated Sole-Soul*; by going through this process, my soul is elevated and ready for my next performance. Let's *goooooooo!*

My prayer is that as you read this book, you will see and discover the flatfooted things that are keeping you from living God's best for you. May "The Lord bless thee and keep thee: The Lord make His face shine upon thee, and be gracious unto thee: The Lord lift up His countenance upon thee, and give thee peace" (Numbers 6:24-26, KJV). "Lift up your heads, Oh ye gates! Lift up, you everlasting doors! And the King of glory shall come in. Who is this King of glory? The Lord of hosts, He is the King of glory" (Psalm 24:7-10, NKJV).

Lift up your head and your eyes and elevate your soul!

INTRODUCTION

I would like to invite you to take a journey with me. I believe the Bible to be among the greatest manuscript ever written. I also discovered in my life that movies, especially Disney-like movies, can be one of the most revealing ways to illustrate a reality of our own life. This book, *The Elevated Soul, "You Are More Than What You See,"* I believe was inspired by the Holy Spirit for me to use the truth of the Scriptures and make a parallelism of one of the all-time great movies and most people favorite movie of all time called *The Lion King.* In this book, I paint a fascinating picture for you of how our lives compare to the life of the little lion called Simba. There is a strong parallel to our lives and an enemy who tells us a lie that causes us to run from our purpose in who God made us to be.

In the movie *The Lion King*, we find little Simba, a lion cub who wanted to be brave and prove to himself, his father, and his uncle, Scar, that he was ready to be king. This act of bravery led to Simba's disobedience and forced him to run away from his pride land because of his father's accidental death. Unfortunately, accidents and situations happen in our lives to where our system is shocked emotionally, spiritually, and physically, and

19

we wonder what to do next. Simba found himself in this position; unfortunately, he listens to the voice of what I call a *lying king* in his uncle Scar. Scar blames little Simba for his father's death and tells little Simba, "Run away Simba, run away and never return." How familiar is this voice that perhaps you have heard in your ears and in your mind and felt in your soul the lie of the enemy when things have gone wrong in your life because of a bad choice or disobedience, and you run away from the purpose in which God created you? Like little Simba, I believe we all can identify with making mistakes in our life or experiencing pain and disappointments from others that put us in a position where we run away from who God created us to be.

In this wonderful movie, Simba was once shown the pride lands by his father Mufasa, who told Simba, "One day all of this would be yours, one day you will be king and rule at all." I believe our Father in heaven has given us power and dominion over all things through the Holy Spirit from the time we were born and from the creation of this world. But something happened along the way in life that causes us to shift our focus from living the life that God has called us to live to running and living in a place where we do not know who we are. Like little Simba, he runs away and does not know that he is a lion, and he finds himself living way below what once was expected of him. A once

chosen little lion cub, now blinded by life's circumstances
and does not realize the power he possesses as a lion, the
king of the jungle. Simba loses himself so much that even
when told by a very dear friend name Nyla that he is the
king, he denied who he was. Greater than that, Simba is
carrying and living with so much shame that when Nyla
tells him his mother would be so proud to see him and
would be so happy that he is alive, Simba's response was,
"Please don't tell her I'm alive."

I believe that many of us have run from the calling
on our lives because of painful experiences, because of
heartfelt disappointments, and we find ourselves hopeless
to the point where we do not know who we are, and we
are living with such shame that we don't want anyone
else to know we are alive. It is not until one day God
sends someone our way to convince us that we have a
greater purpose beyond our pain. In this wonderful movie,
a little monkey named Rafiki shows up on the scene,
and he tells Simba what I think many of us are or have
experienced, which is, "Boy, you don't know who you
are!" A stunning yet funny and fascinating revelation that a
stranger challenged Simba about who he is. But it does not
stop there. Rafiki, the monkey, tells Simba, "I know your
father," in which he gets Simba's attention, yet his attention
was one of disappointment because Simba's response was

"My father is dead," and Rafiki responds, "He's alive; I'll show you!"

Something hit me like a punch in my gut. I can remember the first time I saw this movie, something struck me in my spirit. It occurred to me, and the reason why I was inspired to write this book is that I immediately thought about how many of us are living our lives like we serve and worship a dead father. When I think of a dead father, I am thinking of the powerless Jesus who died on the cross, and yet we read in the Scriptures time and time again that He died and rose again, and He sits on the right hand of God interceding on our behalf. Yet we live our lives like He is still dead, and I am here to tell you He's alive, He's alive, and He desires to do great and mighty things in your life. Our Father in heaven is alive forevermore, and He sits with all power in His hand, and He knows just where you are, and He desires to use the pain of your past for a greater purpose. No matter what has happened to you or what you have been through, God can and will restore you. He will elevate your soul.

And the closing of the same Rafiki takes Simba down to a brook of water, and he tells him he is down there. Simba looks in the water, and he sees a reflection—a reflection of himself—and he responds, "It's just me." Rafiki tells him,

Introduction

"Look harder." Simba looked harder, and this reflection of his father appears. What a wonderful, wonderful illustration; when we look harder in our own life, we will find that we don't just see ourselves, but we see our father who lives in us. Rafiki tells Simba, "You see, he lives in you." Scripture tells us that it is Christ in us that is the hope of glory and that we were made in His image; we are His creation and His workmanship. In Him, we live, we move, and we have our being. It is Christ in us that is the hope of glory. So yes, we will go through pain and disappointment; we may even make bad choices that result in challenging circumstances, but God said, "I will never leave you nor forsake you" (Hebrews 13:5, NKJV), neither height nor depth nor principalities nothing can separate us from the love of God (Romans 8:38-39).

Rafiki and Simba conclude this climactic scene as Simba sees his father in him, an appearance from his father appears in the sky, and his father says, "Remember who you are, you are the son of a king; remember who you are." What a powerful illustration of what God says to us; we are a child of God, we are the son of the one true king in Jesus. We are children of God; remember who you are and never forget that no matter what you are going through or have gone through—remember! Rafiki closes the scene by making a declaration for a lesson we can learn. Rafiki hits

23

Simba over the head, and Simba says, "Ouch, that hurt; why did you hit me?" Rafiki says, "Ahhhh, yeaaa, the past does hurt, but the way I see it, you can either *learn* from it or *run* from it." He swings again, and Simba ducks, and Rafiki says, "You see?" and Simba gets the picture.

Are you living with the pain of your past hurts? Is your painful past weighing you down? I suggest you lay it all down at the feet of Jesus. Put your faith, hope, and trust in the one who loves you and created you. *The Elevated Soul "You Are More Than What You See"* reflects the Scripture Psalm 121:1-2 (NIV): "I lift up my eyes to the mountains—where does my help come from? My help comes from the Lord, the Maker of heaven and earth."

Like Simba, who ran back to take his place and fulfill his purpose, you can too. Run back to God and begin to fulfill your purpose in who he made you to be. Will you take this journey with me through this wonderful book, *The Elevated Soul, "You Are More Than What You See."* You will also experience other fascinating parallels in this wonderful book, where I discuss our five senses and how when we live our lives only by sight and or hearing, we are not experiencing the fullness of what we were created for. God gave us five senses; sight, hearing, taste, touch, and smell. When we make some of life's most critical decisions, we need to utilize all our senses and be in tune with what God has for us. Scripture tells us to taste and see that the Lord is good, smell the aroma of Christ, one touch of the master's hand, my children hear my voice, and I will see the goodness of the Lord in the land of the living. These are five different instances in the Scripture where we are encouraged to use our senses to stay in tune with what God has for us so that we may fulfill His purpose and His calling on her life. I am excited for you to begin to tap into all your senses and elevate your soul. This book covers many different topics I believe we deal with on our journey to finding purpose and fulfillment. As a psychology major in college, God led me to discuss some of the battles of mind, emotional and spiritual battles. I also dive into helping us understand the greatest love of all, the *love of God*, and how love can be manipulated and distorted through the world's view of love.

For those who have broken dreams or feel lost after achieving a dream, I try to help you understand there is a purpose beyond the dreams. I share with you the power of forgiveness, not only understanding God's forgiveness towards us, but also our ability to forgive others and not neglect the most important thing; forgive yourself. Furthermore, this book will help you understand how to exercise your faith, be grateful, and live the life of a true champion. A powerful deep dive into the many things we need in our life to elevate our soul and know we are more than what we see.

YOU ARE MORE THAN WHAT YOU SEE

Welcome to the beginning of a life-changing experience for you; I feel like a kid in the candy store or a kid who just had the best Christmas ever. The revelation of the things that I decided to write in this book gives me great excitement for those of you who read this book. There are topics in this book that were revealed to me as I was rediscovering myself and going through a major transition. The most revealing was I discovered that I am more than what I see or ever saw. I hope you discover and or rediscover who you are and what you were made to be. Let's begin!

Seeing Yourself

Is seeing really believing?

Now faith is the substance of things; hope for the evidence of things not seen!

Fix your eyes on Jesus, the author, and finisher of our faith!

Your eyes have not seen, your ears have not heard neither the things that entered the heart of man! Imagine yourself on the big screen of life, and you are the star of the show! What is it that you see? What role in your movie are you playing? Would your life story involve some pain, heartbreak, being mistreated, abused, rejected, neglected, teased, betrayed, lied on, so much, so you lose sight of who you are?

I would like to introduce to you a startling concept of how do you see yourself? We have been programmed to see everything from the outside, and I believe that concept holds us back from seeing ourselves from the inside out. It is not until you are able to see yourself in the image of something else like the mirror, video, or perhaps a big screen, even better how about seeing yourself in the one that created you. I believe it is in that moment that you begin to see yourself beyond what you see. Our narrow mind and vision of ourselves become limited to our day-to-day environment and surroundings. I encourage you to look beyond that reflection that you see and see the reflection from the one that created you. It is an interesting concept that was also used in the movie *The Lion King*, and for me, I often call it the Lying King (Scar). When Simba lost sight of himself and was not living up to his potential, he was encouraged to look in the water by an old friend and mentor. Simba's first response was the same response I believe most of us would have if someone asked us about ourselves when we are going through a difficult time in our lives. Simba's response was, "I don't see anything but my reflection." Our response is simply from our day-to-day activities, experiences, and surroundings and what we know of ourselves. Rafiki, the monkey, tells Simba, "Look Harder," and as Simba began to see a reflection of his father in himself, Rafiki said to Simba some of the most powerful words we all need to hear; he said, "You see, he lives in you."

Scripture says, "For now we see only a reflection as in a mirror; then we shall see face to face. Now I know in part; then I shall know fully, even as I am fully known" (1 Corinthians13:12, NIV). May I suggest to you that we are more than what we see, especially when we see our Father in heaven in us? It is then that we are "fully known." Our eyesight was not designed to see ourselves further now; it was designed to see only the things God desired for us to see and the things He placed in front of us, but those things that are in front of us were not put there to hinder us, but more so to motivate us, inspire us, to give us knowledge of what it is going to take to become all that we were created to be. In order to do that, we must grasp the concept that "we are more than what we see." In the natural sense, the first thing we do when we face problems is we see the obstacles; we do not immediately think of the solution.

29

What do you think would happen if problems or situations arise and immediately? Our response is, "I may not have the solution to the problem, but I have a relationship with the one who is a problem solver. God, the creator of all things, has the solution to everything we need and want, and in Him and through Him." We can do all things through who strengthens us (Philippians 4:13).

It takes stopping for a moment to process the information before we begin to formulate a solution from the obstacles that are in front of us. I believe many people in life wake up every day, seeing only the things that are in front of them. Our challenge is in order to become the greatest person you can become and achieve the most out of who you are, you must begin to see yourself more than what you see. What do you think would happen if you expand your vision of yourself and broaden your perspective? What if you discovered you could do more, loving and giving more, being more effective in your day-to-day challenges? What if you saw yourself as a winner and not a loser? What if you saw yourself at the top of the mountain instead of in the valley of despair? And, what if you saw yourself as a king or queen and not a servant, an owner and not an employee, an overachiever and not an underachiever? Blessed instead of cursed, happy instead of sad, successful instead of unsuccessful, encouraged instead of discouraged. Ladies and gentlemen, I suggest to you that *you are more than what you see*, and you can experience a great successful, great accomplished thing in this life. I encourage you to see yourself the way your Creator sees you. He sees you as *blessed*, and He loves you! I am my beloved, and He is mine (Song of Solomon 6:3). You are more than what you see!

Seeing Yourself from God's Perspective

It is fascinating that in the Scriptures, God created Adam and Eve without the ability to see or understand one another in an impure or revealing way. It was not until sin entered the world that our eyes open to the differences of who we are and what we see in front of us. We were born with eyes to see things in their purest form, but our eyes have been deceived, diluted, and manipulated that now the first thing we see is the negative in us, the doubt and unbelief in our ability before we are able to see ourselves the way God sees us. So, what is the solution in order to see yourself more than what you see? You need a reflection. I suggest that reflection is in the image of the one who created you. The elevated soul process of sight is that you see yourself the way God sees you. I believe when we begin to do that, we see ourselves more than what we see. This is a transformation process that I believe we all must go through in order to look beyond the natural and begin to see the supernatural.

You may ask yourself well why other people see themselves as successful, productive, and a winner and not a failure. It is my opinion that that happens in our development stage of life. Some people have had the benefit of growing up in a family that helps them see themselves for more than what they see at an early stage. It starts in the home, and perhaps they have been placed in environments such as schools, camps, or something along the way that have reinforced that process of seeing yourself more than what you see. I believe I had this type of experience in my life. In my previous book, *They Call Me Coach*, I explained that it was not until I became a Christian at pistol Pete Maravich basketball camp and relocated into the suburbs of the Johnson family home that I begin to see myself for more than what I used to see. I believe our surroundings, environments, our school systems, our everyday upbringing in our homes, they all shape our sight and program our mind to see the things that we see in life as obstacles or opportunities. For those who grow up and live in an environment or culture that does not see the process of success daily and the necessary character that it takes to be successful, they never began to see themselves as a person of high character or successful; the filter of their eyesight needs to be cleaned. Therefore, they think of themselves based only on what they see. I believe this is a critical process to elevating the soul in your life. It is my contention as a Christian, educator, and influencer that we need to pay more attention to the environment, the cultures, and the surroundings that young people grow up in that ultimately determine the level of achievement or success.

So, you say, why do some like me escape that harsh reality of failure and underachieving? And my response to that would be because something dramatically and drastically changed me and opened my eyes so that I may see things differently. I believe many young people have dreams and goals living in less fortunate situations and desire to be more than what they see, but it appears to me that we have gotten away from helping young people see and believe that they are more than what they see. and present an opportunity to be successful. As I was thinking about this book title, *The Elevated Soul*, it took me to a place of what ultimately elevated my soul. It first began with an opportunity to see something differently. I got a chance to attend a Hall of Fame basketball players camp and see him and hear him and his story, his journey, which ultimately opened my eyes to something more than what I saw before. The thing that I believe costs most people the opportunity to ultimately see themselves the way God sees them and see themselves beyond who they are is the choices we make—but I believe those choices are most of the time a result of what we have seen in our lives.

The power of seeing causes the mind to formulate thoughts of choices that we ultimately make that either propel us to be successful or hinder us from being successful. My challenge to you is to begin to see yourself for more than what you see daily. Begin to look around you and see beyond the circumstances and surroundings that your environment and your culture provide. My prayer is that you can begin to see beyond those things. You are more than what you see, and God has a tremendous purpose and a plan for your life, but He has to become your mirror of reflection that you began to see yourself the way He sees you. You begin to submit and surrender your life to Him and live the life that He has for you, the purpose and the plan that he has for you. He desires to bless you, to give you the abundance of life that you so desire, but you do not get to experience it because you are held back by what you see.

There is a loving God who desires to elevate your soul to new levels and cause you to see things more than what you see. He desires to lift you up on eagle's wings that you may sore at the highest level and achieve the greatest things. You are more than what you see. I encourage you that as you continue your journey in your life, that you allow God to elevate your soul through the process of seeing yourself more than what you see. I encourage you to submit your life to Him and allow for Him to lead you and guide and direct you on the path that He desires for you. He will place opportunities on your way; some of those opportunities may not come in the form of fashion in which you think because your thinking has been a process and a reflection of your current circumstances and the environment and surrounding in which you live. The elevated soul process of life through seeing is to allow a transformation of your heart, your mind, and your soul to be led by the one who created you. As a testimony, I can tell you that Stephon Leary never saw himself as a bestselling author, a coach, a teacher, a school counselor, an inventor, a business owner, a motivational speaker. Nor did I even see myself having the kind of impact on people's lives that I have been so blessed to have experienced.

Sight is a choice; most people have willful blindness or blind spots. They choose not to look at the things that they do not care about and the things they do not want to deal with. I am reminded of the late great Helen Keller, who says: "The only thing worse than being blind is having sight with no vision."

The Elevated Soul

We get so focused on what we are living in that we cannot see what we are looking at and what we were created for. What you hope for and dream for is already there; you just have to see it and embrace it.

The Beginning

I mentioned earlier in this chapter one of the most amazing movies made of all time, in my opinion, is *The Lion King*. A movie that Walt Disney created that gives us an illustration of what happens in our lives when we face devastation and how it affects our lives and ability to see ourselves the way we're created to be—I love *The Lion King*—I see so much of myself in that movie, and I see so much of you in that movie. Perhaps the most powerful scene is the illustration of a totally and completely lost lion cub named Simba, who finds himself living in a world that was not created for him. As you recall in the movie, it was poignant that his father Mufasa took him on a walk one day to show him all that he owned and all that will belong to Simba one day when he becomes king. Once again, proving we are a product of our environment and the things we see in our early stages of life. I can remember that scene in the movie when Simba was so excited to see all the pride land his dad showed him, and in a moment of time, all that there was for him to own, nurture, and grow was a loss. Many times in our lives, we face devastation as Simba did, the loss of a loved one (his father) on a pure accident, materialized from a bad decision, and a lie. However, when those accidents happen in our lives, those failures, those disappointments, the neglect, the rejection, just like in the movie *The Lion King,* there is an enemy of our soul that lies to us and tells us to run away to something else.

The enemy tells us what happens is because of our decisions, and now we are no longer fit to be that which God created us to be. However, that is not the way it works, ladies and gentlemen. The Scripture tells us that if we confess our sins one to another and unto God, He is faithful and just to forgive us of every single solitary sin. It also tells us that God cast is our sin down to the bottom of the sea, and as far as the East is to the West, He remembers them no more. There is always more in you to see even beyond the devastation, the trauma, and the pain that we have experienced in our lives. God has a greater purpose for you beyond those circumstances; you must see yourself for more than what you see during your problems. I want to take it a step further to illustrate to you the power behind seeing yourself the way your true friends and family see you, seeing yourself the way mentors, coaches, and teachers see you and seeing yourself, most of all, the way your Creator God in heaven sees you.

Running Away

Simba runs away; he ends up in a place that is so unfamiliar to him that he does not even realize who he is. Can you identify with that? I can! Simba is greeted by two characters, two complete strangers that become friends; a pig named Pumba and a meerkat named Timon. At first glance, the meerkat and a pig, Pumba and Timon, are afraid because they fear Simba, who is a lion and king of the jungle. Isn't it fascinating that we lose ourselves so much that we do not see who we are, and other people do, and they fear us, but because we do not see ourselves, we fear them? When we run from something to something else, we lose ourselves and do not know who we are. Young Simba was afraid of a meerkat and a pig. It is not so much that he was afraid of them, but it is the thought that a spirit of fear came upon him.

He once was a prideful little lion who was destined for greatness, who wanted to be king, now became a fearful little lion who did not know who he was. How many of you can identify with this? Because of tragedy in your life, you have run from who you are supposed to be, and a spirit of fear is keeping you from seeing yourself for who you were meant to be. I know Stephon Leary can identify. How many

of you can identify with this? As the story continues and a
meerkat and a pig realize that Simba is just a friendly little
lion, they had an *aha* moment that what if they become
friends with this animal, the lion who one day may realize
who he is and everyone else would be afraid of him, he
would be their friend, and he would protect them. Smart
animals, lol, even they knew one day Simba would grow up
and be a big, bold and audacious lion. What about Simba?
What did Simba think of Simba? I laugh at the thought of
this because if I can just get you to see that you are more
than what you see, the world would be put on notice.

Other people see greatness in you; your parents see
greatness in you; your teachers, your coaches, pastors,
youth pastors, and mentors see greatness in you. If and
only if I can just get you to take the blinders off your eyes
and see yourself the way God created you. You would
understand that beyond your circumstances, your past
mistakes, your failures, your disappointments, and your
tragedy, God has a purpose and a plan for your life. What
an amazing story Disney created that I believe gives
us intricate details of what our lives look like as we go
through this thing called the circle of life. The beauty of it
is the day when we come to the realization that we are more
than what we see; it is the most beautiful day. The angels
and people of God celebrate your day of reckoning. "In

the same way, I tell you, there is rejoicing in the presence of the angels of God over one sinner who repents" (Luke 15:10, NIV).

The great Mark Twain wrote, "The two most important days in our lives are the day we were born, and the day we find out why." The time is now for you. The time is now "de carpe diem" seize the moment. Your best life is yet to come. Take your place in this world; what God has for you is reserved for you; no one else can take it. It is up to you to go take your place in this world. Unfortunately, I lost a brother who had become homeless. The sad thing is as I reflect on the life of my brother, Billy Johnson, is when I was adopted into the family. I always thought he was one of the most talented people I ever met. Mind you, I was a talented athlete myself, having played all sports throughout my high school years and obtained a college scholarship to play basketball, and made an attempt to play professional basketball. I thought at Billy's age when I met him; he was destined for greatness. Billy had been shown the great things he could have achieved through a loving mother and father in Dave and Lynne Johnson. The amount of love, support, and guidance was clear from the first time I walked into their home. This was consistent with each kid. In my adopted family, I had two other brothers Jacob and Scott Johnson, who were talented as well, but not as gifted.

You Are More Than What You See

Yet Jacob was exceptionally smart and worked extremely hard and made himself a good basketball player and has become a phenomenally successful professional. Then there was Scott, who was talented as well, he and Billy were biological brothers, so I guess it was in their genes, but Scott did not enjoy sports, so his talent never manifested into anything. Billy, however, could skateboard without lessons; he could jump on the skis on a lake without any lessons. He played basketball, and just about anything he attempted to do, it seemed as if it came natural to him.

To think that he got to a place where he was homeless and died in an alley breaks my heart even today. How could he have lost sight of himself to where he never turned his life around deeply saddens me (Rest in heavenly peace, little brother). My sadness over his life compels me to beg you do not let life beat you up and get you down to where you lose sight of who you are and, most of all, who God is. It makes me wonder how many, just how many homeless people who were destined for greatness who are talented beyond what they see are lost behind tragedy or unfortunate circumstances, or pain or failure. I wonder how many of you are lost, perhaps homeless, because of your past failures and difficult experiences, and because of this, you cannot see who you were created to be. In my two families I have five brothers and one sister in my biological family, and three brothers and one sister in my adopted family, and I wonder how many of us have been affected by things that happened in our life that keeps us from seeing ourselves the way God sees us. You can turn it around if you see yourself more than what you see daily and begin to see yourself the way others see you and, most of all, the way God sees you.

Confronted by a Friend

As Timon and Pumba watch and witness this little lion growing up to be such a huge animal who was destined for greatness, they enjoyed his journey more so than he enjoyed the journey because he did not know who he was, and he could not see himself the way they saw him. In another scene in the movie, Simba's longtime friend, a female lion named Nyla, stumbles upon the scene accidentally looking for food, and ironically, she was chasing after Simba's friend Pumba only to run into her longtime friend Simba. Nyla was born in the same litter as Simba, and the two of them, in their early years, ran off to see and discover all that belonged to Simba as the son of the king who would inherit the pride land one day.

Nyla knew firsthand the greatness in which Simba was created. Sometimes in our lives, when we get lost, it takes friends, true friends, to help us see the greatness in us.

You Are More Than What You See

There is a beautiful song in the movie called *Can you feel the love tonight*. In this song, there are some keywords that Nyla expresses as they wander around laughing and joking, rediscovering their friendship. There is a phrase in the song that says, "Why won't he be the king I know he is, the king I see inside of him?"—*Wow!*

How many frustrated parents, teachers, friends, and coaches looked at you in frustration and said, "why won't you be the king they know you are?" You see, the confusing thing was Nala did not understand why Simba did not see himself as a king anymore, but that was because she was not aware of the tragedy that happened in his life. Sometimes, we do not know what other people are going through, and we have this expectation that sometimes not only frustrates us but frustrates them. Simba struggled with revealing what happened in his past that he was holding onto so much so that he did not want Nala to even let his mom know he was alive. Can you imagine sometimes in our lives, we get to the point where the people we love the most, we do not even want them to know that we are alive or our current situation. We suppress our feelings and emotions and our pain so far down that we do not have the power or the courage to get beyond whatever hurt or devastation and trauma that happened in our lives. I suggest that there is nothing, absolutely nothing, that can separate you from the love of God. No matter what you have done in your life, no matter what your experiences have been in your life, no matter what bad choice you made or what may have happened to you, God still loves you, and He longs to use you in this world. Do not give up on yourself, don't give up on God-don't give up.

There are people who love you, and there are people who need you. Your life matters: you must see yourself for more than what you see. As this wonderful movie continues, in the next scene, Simba finds himself frustrated, disgusted, and confused about who he is.

Facing Your Past

So, he wandered off away from Nyla and his friends Timon and Pumba in disgust, He drop-down in despair but unfortunately, as he dropped furs off, his lion coat floated off him, and my favorite character re-enters the movie—a monkey named Rafiki—who was the one who blessed Simba as he entered the world and anointed him as the next king of the pride land. Rafiki caught wind of the furs and did his little magic potion and painted a mural of what looks like Simba, and in astonishment and complete joy, he said, "Simba, Simba he's alive he's alive 'it is time.'" Just like God, he gave Rafiki an image of what Simba looked like. Again, proving God will send others your way who will try and help you see yourself for who you are. What I love most about this scene is there are times in our lives that our friends try, but cannot convince us who we are and who we are supposed to be, so God brings someone into our life to help us understand who we are and who we were created to be. This person often comes into our lives in the form of a coach, a teacher, a pastor, a mentor, or even perhaps someone who nurtured us while we were young and knew what our place in this world was supposed to look like.

The most powerful and most fascinating thing as it relates to this chapter in this book, "you are more than what you see," is when Rafiki finds Simba. Rafiki finds Simba in a moment of despair and discouragement. Hence, he found him while *his soul was down* or *flatfooted!* How many of you can relate to that, that place where it seems like there is no hope? That place where you are so lost and so confused you do not know how to continue the journey. Unfortunately, I believe that every single one of us comes to this place for a short time, and many of us arrive at this place with more baggage than others, and therefore, some do not remain in that state that others do. My heart's desire as I wrote this book was to help you see what God sees in you. That if I can help you see yourself the way others see you, you will not remain in that state of despair

and discouragement and hopelessness too long either.
My greatest desire in writing this book is that you be set free.
Free to re-enter this world with confidence, wholeness, and
a belief that God has a purpose and a plan for you that far
exceeds what you ever could've imagined. As this powerful
scene of Rafiki and his encounter with Simba ensues, Rafiki
approaches Simba and tells him, "I know who you are,"—
love it—and Simba replies, "You do?" Rafiki then says, "I
know your father," and Simba replies again, "you do?" In
complete shock and sadness, Simba replies again and says,
"Well, my father is dead; he died a long time ago." Rafiki
replies in laughter correction, "He's not dead. He's alive; I'll
show you!" I do not know about you, but as a believer in
Christ, as I watch this scene evolve, it gave me goosebumps.

If you have seen this movie, it gave me chills in
knowing that some people live their lives thinking of the
Christ that is still on the cross and is dead, yet we read
in the Scriptures that Jesus is alive. He rose again on the
third day and reappeared to the disciples perform miracles,
finished his course, ascended to heaven, and now sits on
the right hand of God, and He is interceding for us. He is
alive! "But God raised him from the dead, freeing him from
the agony of death, because it was impossible for death
to keep its hold on him" (Acts 2:24, NIV). I love what
one translation says the grave could not hold him down—

yessss! We do not have to be held *"down"* in our lives; God can and will raise us up! Amen!

We must change our perspective in our moments of despair and times of weakness, helplessness, hopelessness, and understand that the God that created us is alive and He loves us, and He longs for us to return to a place where we acknowledge who He is so that He can use us and our painful past. You see, in Romans 8:28, it says that we know that all things work together for good for those who love the Lord and are called according to his purpose. God has a purpose for your life, and there is nothing that can keep you from that except for you. He will take all the pain of your past and use it for good if you allow Him to. I do not care how bad your life looks right now, and that is all you can see; I'm here to tell you, you are more than what you see.

I am reminded of this beautiful worship song written by Michael W Smith, "Open the Eyes of My Heart" there are a few powerful verses that illustrate the blindness not only in our eyes but in our hearts because of the suffering we have endured. The song says,

"Open the eyes of my heart, Lord

Open the eyes of my heart I want to see

You, I want to see you, to see you high and lifted up

Shinin' in the light of Your glory

Pour out Your power and love

As we sing holy, holy, holy."

Seeing Your Reflection

My prayer is that you see your Father in heaven during your situation. See Him high and lifted up, longing to save you. As this scene continues, Simba doubts Rafiki acknowledging that his father is alive, and so he tells him, "He's over the follow Rafiki, I show you." Rafiki takes Simba to a lake where he tells him, "He's down there," and as Simba slowly takes steps toward looking in the lake, he sees a reflection, and he responds to Rafiki, "I don't see anything. It's just my reflection." If you do not get anything else out of this book or out of this chapter, this is the one thing that I want you to understand. When I thought of writing this book, I began to think how many people wake up every morning, and the first reflection that they see when they look in the mirror is themselves, and you question who you are and doubt your very existence. What is it that you see? For some, the first thing we see is our desolate environment, and we cannot see how we are going to make it. I know the answer will vary because depending on where we are in our lives, what experiences we have had in our life, and what pain we are carrying with us will determine what we see. I also began to think how many of us are living our lives at a low point because we do not see ourselves the way God sees us or the way our friends, family members, and mentors see us. My heart breaks for you at this moment that I am writing this book. I believe many of us look in the mirror, and we see the pain and anguish of our past, and we put on a mask every day just to survive the day, or we see our current situation and how difficult and hopeless it may be. I want you to know God is looking at you; you must look at Him and to Him and see yourself in Him.

In continuance of this wonderful, amazing story of a lion cub who was born to be a king but struggled to see himself the way others saw him and the way his father saw him. Rafiki tells Simba, "Look harderrrr!" I would like to say the same thing to you, look harder; there is more to you than what you see. Look beyond the painful experiences, the hurtful and devastating moments, the failed attempts to fulfilling your dreams and your goals, and know that there is something still great in you. At the moment that Simba look harder, and he saw the reflection of his father in him—what a powerful, powerful, powerful moment that in a time where we look hard enough, we can see our Father in heaven in us. The Scripture tells us that God lives within us. It is Christ in you that is the hope of glory. Second Corinthians 3:18 (KJ21) says, "But we all, with uncovered face beholding as in a glass the glory of the Lord, are changed into the same image, from glory to glory, even as by the Spirit of the Lord."

My prayer is that you would look harder and see the image of Christ in you! As this beautiful scene continues, Mufasa, Simba's father, appears in the sky and in a concerning loving voice, tells him something we all can learn from; he says, "You have forgotten who you are, and so have you forgotten me. Remember who you are!"

My friends, could it be that you have forgotten who you are and so forgotten the God that loves you? Have you reached that point that you forgot who you were created to be that has you living the life you are living? Have you allowed the circumstances of this life to lead you to a place of the unknown? Could it be that you are living in a place where you have settled for less because you have lost sight of who you are? I encourage you as Mufasa encourages Simba, "Remember who you are!" You are a child of God! Bought with a price and born with a purpose as Jeremiah 29:11 (NIV) says, "For I know the plans that I have for you declares the Lord plans to prosper you, to give you hope, to give you a future, and not to harm you." Your life's not over; there's so much more for you to accomplish and achieve. There are so many people who need you!

In conclusion of this wonderful story, Mufasa tells Simba, "You must take your place in this circle of life." Simba, in despair, responded to Mufasa, "You don't know what I've done. I can't go back to be king because of my past." Is this you? Is this why you are settling? Do not believe the lie of the enemy who is trying to rob you of your place in this life. Are you allowing the shame of your past to keep you in bondage from experiencing the life that God has for you? I challenge you to set yourself free and take your place in the circle of life. No matter what you have done, no matter what has happened to you, God has a place for you that only you can take. No one else can take your place; it is a spot that is reserved just for you. You must get up and dust yourself off. Settle within yourself once and for all; you are not gonna allow opinions and thoughts of what someone else thinks to keep you from your destiny. There are still seeds of greatness inside of you; it's up to you to grow into it. Do me a favor take your place in this life! God is waiting on you! Your opportunity to be God's king, God's queen, God's son, God's daughter, is waiting on you.

Every opportunity you desire is waiting on you! I beg of you to see yourself the way God sees you. *You are more than what you see!* In the movie, Simba gets a revelation from Rafiki about his past, and Rafiki says, "You can either learn from it or run from it!" It's your choice, what will you choose to do? You can either remain where you are and run from your past, or you can wake up, get up and learn from your past and become all that God created you to be. You can do it! You do not have to remain in that state or situation you find yourself in. Learn from it and go take your place. This beautiful movie of *The Lion King* gives us a recipe to follow when we lose sight of who we are and run to a place of unfamiliarity and find ourselves lost, confused, depressed, and living below our means.

1. Look Harder—there's more to you than what you see! God has gifted you with gifts and talents you have yet to discover.

2. Remember who you are—you are a child of God; He loves you.

3. Take your place—there's a king, a queen, a son, and a daughter in you that God has a purpose and a plan for your life.

4. Learn from your past—learn and grow from every experience. God will use you and your past to accomplish His will for you.

First Corinthians 2:9 (KJV) says, "But as it is written, Eye hath not seen, nor ear heard, neither have entered into the heart of man, the things which God hath prepared for them that love him."

Transition

Simba ran back to take his place and ran back to a place that could be considered a pandemic. The pride land had become desolate. I want to encourage you when you decide to take your place, you will be faced with a major transition. But if God is for us, who or what can be against us (Romans 8:31). Your transition is the beginning stage of discovering the greatness in you. For many of us, 2020 was a year of freedom and transition of opportunity. A lot was thrown at us and exposed us. For some, it exposed our strengths, and for some, it exposed our weaknesses, and in both situations, there is a change taking place. We got a chance to see ourselves and evaluate our circumstances. God allowed for a pause in life, a temporary shutdown so we can all look introspectively in order to reach new levels. When our computers and our technical devices shut down on us, we take them in for a repair, an upgrade, or buy a new one. I believe 2020 gave us an opportunity to evaluate whether we will remain in our current circumstances and see ourselves where we are, and determine whether it is time for a change, perhaps some repairs, an upgrade, or time for something new. I realized personally in my life I have been in love with this game that I sometimes call my girlfriend "Basketball." This was an undying love that I have had for most of my life as a player and as a coach. I realize in the pandemic, for me, it was time for something new. Often when we go through these changes in our lives, it's difficult; it presents new problems and challenges that we don't yet have solutions for, and we battle emotional challenges of fear and anxiety, and sometimes depression, but the key is knowing that God will take you through if you trust and believe in Him.

I love the concept of the butterfly caterpillar transformation. For some of us, we began this transition from our caterpillar stage of crawling on things to flying and finding the beauty within us—that has a greater purpose. In this transition, things are falling off you, and some things are growing on you; your wings—and it's not pretty and very difficult. I am sure when caterpillar, if they have a chance to look in the mirror and the transition stage, probably would not think very highly of itself either laughing out loud. Think about it; the caterpillar has this strange sack on it, and it is bursting out of. I would imagine at that moment, the caterpillar/butterfly is incapable of doing not much. Perhaps this may be you.

You Are More Than What You See

God is forming you and transitioning you into something for a greater purpose. It is extremely important that you see yourself the way God sees you and not lose sight of who you are and what you were created to be. Do not be so quick to want more, or it will slow your wings from producing, and you will not be able to fly. This transition may require being alone, or you will let things in your life that will weigh you down. Do not run back to crawling because of relationships or dependence on someone or things. Be freeeeee! You are about to fly high, so be patient. The people and things God has for you are up higher, not on the level you are! What you see now, you will rise above soon! You were a great caterpillar, but you are going to be an even greater butterfly. First Corinthians 2:9 (KJ21) says, "But as it is written, Eye hath not seen, nor ear heard, neither have entered into the heart of man, the things which God hath prepared for them that love him."

You got to know that when God is taking you to new levels, there will not be many people around. As the elevator goes up, only the select few can go to the top. A famous quote for Dr. Martin Luther King is, "You don't have to see the whole staircase, just take the first step," and I say wherever you are on your stairs, keep stepping up. God is taking you places where others cannot go with you. The key to understand is that when you get to the top, keep in mind;

55

God took you there, give Him the glory and go back and help others reach the top. Your life of success and or prosperity is not just for you; it is for you to use that stage and platform to bring others along with you. Isaiah 55:9 (ASV) says, "For as the heavens are higher than the earth, so are my ways higher than your ways, and my thoughts than your thoughts."

We are only capable of processing information on our human level, but God's thoughts and purpose and plan for us is something we cannot comprehend, and the only way we can ever see what He has in store for us is to seek Him, to get to know Him on His level through praise, prayer, service, and worship. Submit our lives for a greater purpose. We sometimes lose sight of who we are because we find more comfort in food, alcohol, drugs, sex, and other things. I came across a remarkably interesting story in the Scriptures in Isaiah, where he describes what wine and alcohol can do to alter your state, and you find yourself trying to make the best decision for your life or dream decisions.

An interesting verse in the Scriptures that talks about being able to see after having consumed wine and beer is Isaiah 28:7 (NIV); it says, "And these also stagger from wine and reel from beer: priest and prophets stagger from beer and are befuddled with wine; they reel from beer they stagger when seeing visions, they stumble when rendering decisions."

You Are More Than What You See

Perhaps this can serve as not only a directive to what overconsumption of beer and wine does to us when we try and "see" things properly to make good decisions. Maybe this is a great way to look at the things in our life that alter our ability to see ourselves clearly or to see ourselves the way our Father in heaven sees us. I believe there are many things that happen or incur in our lives through abuse, mistreatment, failure, disappointments that alter our ability to see. I realize it is easy to say that about those who partake in substances, but what is keeping the rest of us from seeing ourselves clearly and seeing the possibilities beyond our daily experiences.

The Elevated Soul of *"you are more than what you see"* is (Ephesians 3:20) now to him who is able to do immeasurably more than all we ask or imagine, according to his power that is at work within us. If we truly submit our lives to Christ, He elevates our souls and promises to give us everything we need. He promises that He will never leave us or forsake us. So, in those times where we, like Simba, run from something or hide from the pain of our past or suppress the pain of something that did not go well for us, we have to know and understand God is still with you and he's waiting for you to come home.

I recall the story in the Scripture Luke 11 where Jesus

tells a story of the prodigal son. Like Simba, he ran off to a faraway place and squandered all of his wealth and earning that his father bestowed upon him, seeking to find fulfillment in the world that left him in a place where he was feeding the pigs in mud and so hungry that he wanted to eat their food; he had no place to go no food to eat, nowhere to live. Luke 15:17-19 (NIV):

> When he came to his senses, he said, "How many of my father's hired servants have food to spare, and here I am starving to death! I will set out and go back to my father and say to him: Father, I have sinned against heaven and against you. I am no longer worthy to be called your son; make me like one of your hired servants."

This is a story that many of us can relate to, that we get angry, frustrated, confused, bruise beyond what we think can be repaired, and we run to the world looking for healing, and because we forget who we are and forget who God is and us that we don't realize the one who can heal us is within us. God is a healer. He loves us. He created us. He longs to have fellowship with us. The beauty of the story of the prodigal son is that the Bible says, "and when he came to his senses,"—what a powerful, powerful state to be in. You see, it's that moment and time in our lives where we have what I call *the great awakening*. Many people call it other things, the great motivational speaker, Tony Robbins, described it as a "breakthrough."

The amazing Christian artist Kirk Franklin wrote a song called "Imagine Me" in 2005. In the song, he describes an imagination of being free from all the things that have held us back. But he starts this song with what I think is one of the most powerful things we can do, and that is he says in a little prayer, "Thank you for allowing me to see myself the way you see me!" I believe when we reached the point where we can get past all of our pain, insecurities, brokenness, shame, and failure and *see ourselves the way God sees us, we truly become free!* The challenge in our lives is to understand that life happens, and through everything that goes on this journey to fulfill our purpose in this life, God is with us, and He longs for the opportunity to use us for a greater purpose. You are more than what you see! It doesn't matter what you've done; if you can begin to look up and see yourself the way God sees, you can begin to walk out of all of the pain and suffering over the many years and find true meaning in the loving arms of our Savior and Creator Jesus Christ.

If I could tell everyone in this world who may struggle with insecure thoughts and feeling insignificant, it is whenever you get up in the morning and see yourself, see yourself the way God sees you. Flip the God switch on and begin to see yourself the way God sees you. There is another revealing verse in this wonderful song Kirk Franklin wrote many years ago, and that is my hope and prayer for you that one day you can have the attitude that Kirk Franklin expresses in this song. Here it is. I hope you become free,

"Imagine me

Loving what I see when the mirror looks at me 'cause I

I imagine me

In a place of no insecurities

And I'm finally happy 'cause

I imagine me

Letting go of all of the ones who hurt me

'Cause they never did deserve me

Can you imagine me?

Saying "No" to thoughts that try to control me

Remembering all you told me

Lord, can you imagine me?"

You Are More Than What You See!

EMOTIONAL AND SPIRITUAL CLOTS

When we reach a certain age or time in our life, we have to go get a sonogram or angiogram. An *angiogram* is a diagnostic test that uses X-rays to take pictures of your blood vessels. A long flexible catheter is inserted through the bloodstream to deliver dye (contrast agent) into the arteries making them visible on the x-ray. A sonogram is an image produced by ultrasound. This sonogram reveals the things underneath the surface of our outward appearance. So often, a healthy individual looks like they have life altogether on the outside; however, some of the most detrimental things can be revealed when we get a physical sonogram. So, then there is an angiogram which is used to see pictures of your blood vessels and arteries. So many people, unfortunately, slowly over time develop unknown "Blood Clots." This is extremely dangerous because blood clots; while many people know that a heart attack is the number one cardiovascular threat and stroke is threat number two, too few people do know about the number three cardiovascular killer—venous thromboembolism (VTE) or a blood clot found mostly in the leg and lungs—and its consequences. Many doctors do not diagnose it early enough to prevent or treat it correctly, so too many people are dying from a preventable death. After studying about blood clots and having family members experience blood clots, I realized something; I wonder what would happen if we took a spiritual sonogram and angiogram to get an idea of any possible emotional clots or blockages that may be revealed that keep us from experiencing the freedom, the strength and peace of life that God desires for us.

Could it be that many of us are walking around with "emotional clots" that are keeping the Blood of Jesus from flowing throughout our body, heart, mind, and soul? I challenge you to take a spiritual sonogram to see if there are emotional clots that are blocking the joy of your salvation and freedom in Christ. Scripture tells us to take a test; it is called a "spiritual test," not a sonogram. Not only does Scripture tells us to take a test, but God also tests us as Job describes in Job 7:17-18 (NIV), "What is mankind that you make so much of them, that you give them so much attention, that you examine them every morning and test them every moment?"

One must wonder if God is testing us, how can we know the results of what He sees and what His observation is. Perhaps if we visit God, like we go to visit our doctors, we will know what is happening in our body, heart, soul, and mind. The Scripture tells us that God is the "Good Doctor!" "On hearing this, Jesus said to them, 'It is not the healthy who need a doctor, but the sick. I have not come to call the righteous, but sinners'" (Mark 17, NIV). Are you glad that in Christ we have the best doctor there is to heal us from all our situations? He is the great healer! No matter what your situation is, He desires to heal you, cleanse you, open the flood gates of heaven and bless you. So, do you think you have emotional "clots" that are blocking the flow of God in your life?

The Blood of Jesus

Let us go deeper! While I understand in writing this book, I am writing a chapter on "emotional and spiritual clots," relating it to physical blood clots; it can block the passage for life to flow to the heart and mind that causes us heart attacks and mental breakdowns. What do I mean? Well, I know in my own life I have often wondered why I have these moments where I feel lifeless or unfulfilled. In taking my own test, I began to evaluate my life and ask God, "what is keeping me from finding complete peace, love, and happiness in my life?" As I was going through my journey in creating and inventing my training and rehabilitation boot for the first time in my life, I wanted God to take an inventory of me. Many people thought my discovery and creating the training and rehabilitation boot with the elevated sole was an exhilarating experience. However, what they did not realize was while I was going through that process, God began to elevate my soul because He began to show me areas in my life that had gone unattended. There were many times I had to take long trips to Atlanta and Virginia, back to Liberty University where I was using them to help me come up with a model prototype that I could use in my patent process and begin to think about the manufacture and production of the training and rehabilitation boot. Sure, I thought to myself humbly God had given me something I would have never imagined myself creating and inventing, but most importantly, I began to discover my emotional clots. Many people, including my parents, used to ask me as I was taking these trips to Liberty or Atlanta, "Why aren't you flying?" My response to them was, "I'm going on my God journey," I prefer to drive. Those who know me know I will drive anywhere across the US as opposed to flying.

For me, there was no substitution for listening to inspiring messages, gospel, and praise and worship music while I am traveling. Many times, I broke down in tears as I drove up and down the highway. I realized on these trips it was more about the quality time I could spend with God and let the great physician test and evaluate me. It became noticeably clear to me that I had "emotional and spiritual clots," and I wanted to break free so the joy and happiness that come from the blood of Jesus can *flow* in my life and my life shall be fulfilled. Each time I took a trip, there was a breaking and releasing of revelation into the things that were holding me back. This became a time that I felt alive in Christ and felt the presence of God like never before. I once described these moments to friends and family "It was as if God was sitting in the passenger seat beside me talking me through my internal struggle of the pain of broken relationships, failure, setbacks, my past life of rejection, neglect, and abuse, and my own bad choices." This experience was the seed planted in my mind of now writing a book four years later, calling it *The Elevated Sole-Soul*. So, I ask you, do you have emotional clots/blockages that are keeping you from experiencing the blood of Jesus flowing in your heart, soul, mind, and body that give you the peace, love, and happiness we all long for? You see, what I discovered and had a divine revelation was those emotional clots are things like fear, emotional, physical, and sexual abuse, failure, neglect, rejection, broken relationships, tragedy, church hurt, drug and alcohol dependence.

I began to wonder how many people may not know what is keeping them from finding fulfillment and purpose.

Is it possible they are experiencing "emotional and spiritual clots" and just do not know and now on the verge of a mental breakdown or spiritual heart attack? You will not know what's holding you back or blocking your passages of the blood of Christ to flow in your life until you visit the great physician and allow Him to sit with you and reveal to you where your blockages are and began treatment and healing in you. I am excited for you to take a visit and get your spiritual sonogram. God longs and desires to see you be free from all sin and bondage and be free to experience the life that He has for you. It is essential for us to learn about the importance and meaning of the blood of Jesus. Jesus gave His life and shed His blood to reconcile us from sin if we believe in Him.

"But if we walk in the light, as he is in the light, we have fellowship with one another, and the blood of Jesus his Son cleanses us from all sin" (1 John 1:7, ESV). Jesus demonstrated the significance of His blood as part of the Last Supper with His disciples. As the disciples sat together, Jesus said,

"Take this and eat it, for this is my body." And he took a cup of wine and gave thanks to God for it. He gave it to them and said, "Each of you drink from it, for this is my blood, which confirms the covenant

Emotional and Spiritual Clots

between God and his people. It is poured out as a sacrifice to forgive the sins of many."

Matthew 26:26-28 (NLT)

The blood of Jesus flows in and through us to cleanse us from all unrighteousness. This same blood is your strength and power to overcome all the things that try and block your passage of freedom in Christ. There is a powerful song called "You Are My Strength." I love when Miranda Curtis sings it. The verses are so powerful in our comprehension of the blood of Jesus. It says:

> "The blood that gives me strength
> From day to day
> It will never lose its power
> It reaches to the highest mountain
> It flows to the lowest valley
> The blood that gives me strength
> From day to day
> It will never lose its power."

The blood of Jesus will reach you at your highest point in life and *flow* to the lowest valley, and it will never ever lose its power—wowwww! Can you imagine the blood of Jesus flowing in and through our body, removing every blockage of emotional, spiritual, and even physical

67

pains? It will never lose its power. Are you ready to be heal of what may be blocking your flow? For me, I realize I was experiencing that "perfect storm," the experience of something that happened as a painful experience in my past that somehow showed up in my present life and was magnified when the person you love, or the situation you thought was so perfect for you, came crashing down. The enemy uses these circumstances to create emotional scars that go unattended and later one day are revealed as an emotional clot. That painful and hurtful experience has remained in our bodies for such a long time that it has formed an emotional clot. That clot that says you're not worthy, you're not good enough, you're ugly, you're inadequate, and many of us walk around feeling like we could never be loved again, or we could never achieve great things in our life well no one will ever hire us again.

Emotional clots cause us spiritual clots where we no longer see God as our source of help in a time of need when that is the exact opposite of who God is. We get to such a low place in our lives that we just accept life for what it is and try and manage and do whatever we can to get by from day to day, and I'm here to tell you that God has so much more for you. He wants to release you and to free you from those blockages that are keeping you from smiling again, from loving again, from fulfilling your purpose that He created you to do in your life. It is time for a sonogram, and let God revealed those things that are holding you back. Let the blood of Jesus flow and improve your life, and you will experience great and mighty things.

Scripture says, "How much more, then, will the blood of Christ, who through the eternal Spirit offered himself unblemished to God, cleanse our consciences from acts that lead to death, so that we may serve the living God!" (Hebrews 9:14, NIV). I love this Scripture because it says, "the blood cleanse our conscience from acts that lead to death"—wow! You see, we are living our lives through our limited knowledge and not allowing the Holy Spirit to help us make decisions that lead to life and peace and not death. Scripture tells us life in Christ Jesus will set us free. "Because through Christ Jesus the law of the Spirit who gives life has set you free from the law of sin and death" (Romans 8:2, NIV). Spiritually speaking, you must know the enemy of our souls does not desire to see you and me happy and free of those clots. For me, I am determined to have a purpose fulfilled life! God wants that for us. I continue to repeat throughout this book that the Bible says in John 10:10 (KJV) about the thief cometh not but to steal to kill and destroy, but I have come that you may have life and have it more abundantly! God wants you to live a life of abundance free from those emotional and spiritual clots.

Healing Your Injuries

Ironically as I studied blood clots in the body, I discovered that blood clots can be formed from injury. Isn't that coincidental? An injury in the body causing blood to form a clot over time can be dangerous to the body. I found this fascinating and my comprehension and understanding of how emotional and spiritual clots can be caused by injury. What has injured you that is perhaps causing your clot? That is why we need a sonogram with the great physician so that he can reveal the injuries that are causing a clot in our body. I also found it interesting that one of the most common treatments or remedies for "Blood Clots" is prescribing blood thinners. This process is to reduce the clot thinning out the blood so that the passages are open again for blood to flow in the body. I find this fascinating as I look at Scripture because what Jesus did was take the blow so that his shed blood would lessen the blow for us and open the door of hope for us.

> **For all have sinned and fall short of the glory of God, and all are justified freely by his grace through the redemption that came by Christ Jesus. God presented Christ as a sacrifice of atonement, through the shedding of his blood—to be received by faith. He did this to demonstrate his**

righteousness, because in his forbearance he had left the sins committed beforehand unpunished.

Don't be deceived by your own desires, or your painful past experiences, or the enemy. Let the Word of God dwell in your hearts. Allow His Word to saturate every dry place and thin out every emotional or spiritual clot that is revealed. Let His Word erase the past and transform your present situation and your future. The more you intentionally visit the great healer and physician and focus on living out His Word daily, the more you'll become like Christ, and the blood of Jesus will sustain you in everything you come up against. Surrender to His will, and let your character reflect Him in every aspect of your life, in your relationships, your job, your profession or business, and your friends and family. Do not allow your thoughts to drift to what was and what happened to you; make every effort to dwell on the goodness of God. Scriptures say,

Finally, brothers and sisters, whatever is true, whatever is noble, whatever is right, whatever is pure, whatever is lovely, whatever is admirable— if anything is excellent or praiseworthy—think about such things. Whatever you have learned or received or heard from me or seen in me—put it

into practice. And the God of peace will be with you.

Philippians 4:8-9 (NIV)

Always look to God's Word; His Word is powerful and pierces those pain areas in our lives that may have caused a clot. "For the word of God is alive and active. Sharper than any double-edged sword, it penetrates even to dividing soul and spirit, joints and marrow; it judges the thoughts and attitudes of the heart"

TRIGGERS

Let me define for you the idea of how there are things in our lives that provoke a negative reaction or quick response within our mental and emotional psyche. These reactions often make us respond out of character and sometimes paralyze us from taking actions or attempting things we need to do, and we shut down. Sometimes it causes us to say things and do things we regret later. This can be defined as a "Trigger." In my experience, triggers stem from an underlying painful experience that causes us some level of insecurity. These insecurities cause us to feel like we need to defend ourselves or protect ourselves from ever being hurt again by someone or something. This is a defense mechanism that keeps us from living a life of peace and happiness. It also puts us in a position where we develop an ego that we also use as a weapon to hurt others before they hurt us. If we can learn what those triggers are in our life and allow ourselves to be healed of those painful insecure areas, we will find ourselves more at peace and able to enjoy successful relationships with others and, most importantly, our spouses and the people we love the most. Can you imagine what that would do for all of us? It's important that we all embrace the responsibility to not trigger someone else. That is a mean-spirited tactic that the enemy used to destroy relationships and families.

Once someone knows what our trigger is, a harp on it and calls us hysteria in our own lives. The Scripture is very clear about not focusing on someone's triggers and encourages us to stimulate and encourage one another in love.

> **And let us consider how we may spur one another on toward love and good deeds, not giving up meeting together, as some are in the habit of doing, but encouraging one another—and all the more as you see the Day approaching.**
>
> **Hebrews 10:24-25 (NIV)**

I love how the Scripture not only describes how we should inspire one another but it also gives a picture of what happens when we do not. It says sold that we do not give up on meeting together. What a powerful illustration of what triggering someone leads to. The last part of verse 25 also tells us why we should do this because the days are approaching, meaning we never know when someone's day on this earth will end, even our own, so treat one another with love and encouragement. The last thing that we would want to see happen to someone is that we lose them, and the last words that were spoken to them were triggering them to a negative choice. Let us take a deeper dive into what triggers are and how they affect us.

Recognizing Triggers

What does it mean to be "triggered?" This term has been casually used to refer to the experience of having an emotional reaction to some type of disturbing content (such as violence or the mention of suicide) in the media or in another social setting. However, there is a difference between being triggered and being uncomfortable. Feeling triggered isn't just about something rubbing you the wrong way. For someone with a history of trauma, being around anything that reminds them of a traumatic experience (also known as a "trigger") can make them feel like they're experiencing the trauma all over again. Though commonly used to refer to the experiences of people with post-traumatic stress disorder (PTSD), the term "trigger" can also be used in the context of other mental health illnesses, or individuals who have had some very bad things done to them, or individuals who have been neglected and rejected to the point they feel no sense of worth. This includes substance use disorders, eating disorders, and anxiety. In these cases, a trigger is seen as anything that prompts an increase in or return of symptoms. For example, a person recovering from a substance use disorder may be triggered by seeing someone using their drug of choice. The experience may cause returned cravings and even relapse. It's important that we refrain from the area and things in our life that may trigger us to a negative response. Let us look at the various types of triggers. Triggers vary widely from person to person and can be either internal or external. Below are examples of the different kinds of events that might be considered triggers in terms of mental health problems.

Internal Triggers

An internal trigger comes from within the person. It can be a memory, a physical sensation, or an emotion. For example, say you're exercising, and your heart starts pounding. That sensation might remind you of a time you were running from an abusive person. So internal triggers do not necessarily have to be a direct reflection of what happened to you in the past. This example would be considered an internal trigger. Other common internal triggers include: anger, anxiety, feeling overwhelmed, vulnerable, abandoned, or out of control, loneliness, muscle tension, memories tied to a traumatic event, pain, and sadness. Many of these topics have responses when we feel these emotions internally.

Although sometimes the feelings that we feel may not be from the same person or from the same thing, we are reminded of this emotion when we experience it with someone else, or something else happens that reminds us of what happened in the past. This is very important to know that things in our lives that hold us back from having the kind of positive emotions that we would like to experience from the people we love, our friends, our family our business colleagues and have the confidence to participate in things that will not give us this turn internal feeling. The key is once we define these areas in our lives that we understand that God does not desire nor want us to live under the power of these triggers that we cannot find peace, hope, love, trust, belief, and confidence in ourselves and others.

External Triggers

External Triggers can come from the environment. They can be a person, place, or a specific situation. Think of the impact that a situation such as the 2019-2020 Coronavirus (COVID-19) pandemic may have on those struggling with mental illness. Many may view self-quarantine guidelines and stay-at-home orders as a minor inconvenience. However, someone recovering from a binge eating disorder—a disease that thrives in isolation—

may feel triggered under such circumstances. Some other common things that may cause a person to feel triggered: a movie, television show, or news article that reminds you of the experience, a person connected to the experience, arguing or discussing with a friend, spouse, or partner, a specific time of day. Certain sounds that remind you of the experience (a military veteran might be triggered by loud noises that sound like gunfire) changes to relationships or ending a relationship, significant dates (such as holidays or anniversaries), going to a specific location that reminds them of the experience, smells associated with the experience, such as smoke. Most believe we do not know precisely how triggers are formed. As I studied the topic of triggers, I found that some researchers believe that our brains store memories from a traumatic event differently from memories of a non-traumatic event. Past traumatic events may be interpreted by the brain as current. This causes the body to experience symptoms like the original trauma (such as the fight-or-flight response). Researchers say most people are not even aware of their triggers; they live in the subconscious mind. We also know that triggers can cause an emotional reaction before a person realizes why they have become upset. Often triggers have a strong sensory connection (a sight, sound, taste, or smell) or are connected in some way to a deeply ingrained habit (for example, a recovering alcoholic who associates a particular activity with drinking).

Victory Over Triggers

So, what can we do to deal with or get victory over "Triggers"? As you look at all of the laundry lists of things that internal and external "Triggers" can be and the damage they may cause, we can find peace in knowing number one; you're not alone. A vast number of people deal with some kind of trigger because of our human nature and frailty. However, I can also look at this list and know that Jesus came to this earth specifically for the broken-hearted and the loss. "The Lord is close to the brokenhearted and saves those who are crushed in spirit" (Psalm

Try and replay in our minds and our hearts the words that Christ says about us and those moments of being triggered. We also must listen to the voices of those who love us and think differently about us and those moments. One of the lies of the enemy is to tell you that no one likes you, no one cares about you, no one will ever love you, no one would ever hire you, you're not good enough, for anything or anyone and folks, that's just not true. I felt so compelled to write this chapter because I can identify with that number one but number two because I want for you to understand that there are bigger and better things in store for you beyond the hurt and pain that we may experience and suffer from at the hands of the voice or the situation of someone else. I have shared and said in other chapters in this book how important it is to find a place of solitude and a quiet place not to experience being alone but to get along with God. Somehow, someway, when you are in the presence of God through prayer, praise and worship, and the reading of Scripture's books or things that speak of God's Word, it strengthens to you, it gives you a new perspective, it heals you and helps you forget the hurt that you may have experienced.

I know what you are thinking, but Mr. Stephon Leary, what about when I'm not able to get into that place of solitude or quiet time? I believe the more and more you spend time in these moments, that voice gets louder, and louder, and louder in your mind and your heart and in your soul, that it sustains you throughout the days and weeks and protects you from the harm of others. I know it sounds simple and easy, but it's not; it requires a commitment just like everything else we do in our lives. As a former coach, I used to encourage my players to spend time shooting, dribbling, passing, and learning their role on the team so that it becomes an innate habit. Therefore, when the games and practices come, everything becomes secondhand to you.

Triggers

I believe this can provide a solution for those of us who struggle with certain triggers in our lives. We need to commit to every day and exercise of rebuking and resisting the false voices, sounds, and events that trigger us to feel less than what God created us to be. Scripture tells us in 2 Timothy 1:7 God has not given us a spirit of fear or timidity but of power, love, and a sound mind. We have the power to love; we have the power to not live in timidity or fear; we have the power to think with a sound mind through the spirit of God. How many of us, when we are triggered by something or someone, immediately have a negative response before we think about what God would want us to do. Sometimes we must choose to relax and trust God, relax and find peace on this journey, and understand God's got you. Sometimes we feel the best way for us to protect ourselves is to run and hide, and that running and hiding cost us more pain and anguish. The only hiding place we need is to hide in the presence of God. One of the things I'd like to share with you on how to protect yourself from your triggers is to understand what the Scripture says about putting on the full armor of God. We know that there is an enemy of our soul that desires to not see us live in peace and joy and happiness and hope and service to one another, so we must protect ourselves from him and the best way to do that is to understand the armor that we possess and God.

The Elevated Soul

Here is what the Scripture says about the armor of God,

Finally, be strong in the Lord and in his mighty power. Put on the full armor of God, so that you can take your stand against the devil's schemes. For our struggle is not against flesh and blood, but against the rulers, against the authorities, against the powers of this dark world and against the spiritual forces of evil in the heavenly realms. Therefore, put on the full armor of God, so that when the day of evil comes, you may be able to stand your ground, and after you have done everything, to stand. Stand firm then, with the belt of truth buckled around your waist, with the breastplate of righteousness in place, and with your feet fitted with the readiness that comes from the gospel of peace. In addition to all this, take up the shield of faith, with which you can extinguish all the flaming arrows of the evil one. Take the helmet of salvation and the sword of the Spirit, which is the word of God. And pray in the Spirit on all occasions with all kinds of prayers and requests. With this in mind, be alert and always keep on praying for all the Lord's people.

Ephesians 6:10-18 (NIV)

Wowwwww! Do you see how God laid out for us very specifically and gave direction on its purpose? I don't know about you, but I feel good knowing that I have something to draw towards when I'm being triggered by something or someone. The Word of God tells us that the enemy throws fiery darts at us and the picture that I get is when I have the full armor of God on, I can deflect those things that he is throwing at me. I think of those things as being triggered that something or someone is attempting to ruin my day my mood or possibly hurt me.

The Full Armor of God

Let's go a little deeper on perhaps how we can use the full armor of God.

Belt of Truth: Back in the day, a Roman soldier's belt was made of metal and thick heavy leather and was the carrying place for his sword. It also had a protective piece that hung down in the front. His belt held all other pieces of his armor together; therefore, the truth is the belt that holds our armor together as well. The ultimate truth can only be found in God's Word and in Jesus Christ. We must know this truth in order to protect ourselves against ourselves, the world, and the enemy of our soul, and others who might speak lies to hurt us. The truth grounds us and reminds us of our identity in Christ.

Breastplate of Righteousness: The Roman soldier was always equipped with a breastplate. This piece of armor protected his vital organs in the heat of the battle. As believers, we have no righteousness apart from that which has been given to us by Christ. Our breastplate is supposed to be His righteousness when we choose to do what is right in the eyes of God. Living a right life rooted in God's Word is powerful in protecting our hearts, eliminating our flesh, and defeating the enemy.

Sandals The Gospel of Peace: Roman soldier's feet were fitted with sandals. These sandals were made to help protect soldier's feet. They had extremely thick soles and wrapped perfectly around their ankles in a way that protected against injury. This also helped them have a firm foundation. As believers, we also have a firm foundation in the Gospel. As believers, we have peace in knowing we are secure in what Jesus has done for us (Just as we discussed the importance of our feet as it relates to "Xxcelerator Training and Rehabilitation Boot," God uses our feet to give us a firm foundation.)

Shield of Faith: The Roman soldier's shield was a complex piece of armor. The shield was a soldier's primary defensive weapon. It was made to deflect the fiery arrows of the enemy. Faith is the shield of the believer. Trusting in God's power and protection is the key to overcoming our triggers. When those difficult times arise, we must remember that God works all things for good. He is always true to His promises. We must always have faith in the one that created us.

Helmet of Salvation: The Soldier's head is one of his most vulnerable areas, just like us. Without his helmet, one blow to the head would prove fatal. His helmet covered his entire head, facial area, and between the eyes. The believer's helmet of salvation is the most crucial piece of armor for the Christian. Without the indwelling Holy Spirit that enters a believer at the moment of salvation, all other armor is useless. Salvation empowers believers to know who they are when others speak against them, and it protects us in our weaknesses, especially those things we allow to enter our minds. Without salvation, through Christ, there is no victory. Victory in Jesus!

Sword of the Spirit: All other pieces of the soldier's arsenal are defensive weapons, but not the sword. The sword was a deadly weapon. In the hands of a skilled warrior, he could pierce through even the strongest armor. Our sword is the Word of God, both the written and the

incarnate Word. You must learn to use your sword of the
Spirit. With God's Word, we are truly able to fight and
defeat all enemies. Even Christ Himself used Scripture
to defeat Satan when He was tempted in the desert. We
must do the same. But you must spend time learning the
Scriptures, so you can have them in your mind when others
say things opposite the Scriptures.

Prayer: In prayer, we show our complete dependence
upon God to act and move on our behalf. Our entire armor
is rooted in God's strength, and without His presence, we
are powerless in the fight against the enemy, ourselves,
and all those things that come against us. We must fight on
our knees; our prayer time gives us the strength we need to
carry on. We will see a victory when we fight in His power.

As you look at those seven key things about putting
on the armor of God, maybe you can see how you can
overcome those triggers and not allow those things to keep
us from being all that God has created us to be. Whether
it be internal triggers or external triggers, we still have the
ability to overcome them and not allow them to cause us to
live a defeated life. You are an overcomer! Jesus says, "I
have told you these things, so that in me you may have
peace. In this world you will have trouble. But take heart! I
have overcome the world" (John 16:33, NIV).

We also must realize not everything that happened to us is bad; sometimes, what happens to us is for us. Let me say that again, sometimes what happens to us is for us. God has a greater purpose and using things in our lives to grow as immature as to make us stronger for where he is taking us. Ecclesiastes 3:1 (KJV) states that God has established a time and season for everything: "To everything there is a season, and a time to every purpose under the heaven." When you face those triggers internally or externally, just know that God still has a purpose and a plan for your life. There is no one or nothing that can separate you from the love of God and can keep you from fulfilling the purpose and plan he has for your life. Don't give up on yourself! Don't give something or someone the power over you to keep you from experiencing the blessed life that God has for you. Choose to hold your peace and wait for His season. His timing is perfect. His season is perfect. Choose His peace over your process. His peace will navigate your course. His peace will direct your heart. His peace will direct your path. His peace will keep you. His peace will give you life beyond what you ever could imagine!

Ecclesiastes 3:8 (KJV) also states that there is "A time to love, and a time to hate; a time of war, and a time of peace." Pray and actively choose to rest in His peace. Let God fight your battle. Let God go before you. When it's time to war, God will teach you how to war. When it's time to war, He'll give you the strength and fortitude to fight. When it's time to fight, God will give you the wisdom and insight to conquer the enemy. When it's time to relax, choose to hold on to your peace and trust God—the battle belongs to the Lord. Oftentimes, it takes more strength to restrain yourself than it does to respond. Choose to hold your peace and crucify your flesh. Even as Christ was being crucified, He actively chose not to respond to His persecutors. He chose to hold His peace so that we can have peace. Choose to surrender to God and hold on to His peace. Renew the relationship with your mind and heart. Scripture tells us in Romans 12:1-2,

> **Therefore, I urge you, brothers and sisters, in view of God's mercy, to offer your bodies as a living sacrifice, holy and pleasing to God—this is your true and proper worship. Do not conform to the pattern of this world but be transformed by the renewing of your mind. Then you will be able to test and approve what God's will is—his good, pleasing and perfect will.**

Choose not to allow the triggers in your life to keep you from fulfilling God's good, pleasing, and perfect will. I believe that if we can identify those triggers in our lives from our past pains, failure, rejection, neglect, and the things that happened to us that were not right and not fair, we will recognize those things and allow God to begin to heal us from those things, and put on the full armor of God and choose to live the life that He's called us to live—we can experience an elevated soul by dealing with those triggers.

DREAMS VS. PURPOSE

In this chapter, I would like to open your eyes and
expand your thinking, your vision, and understanding
of the difference between dreams accomplished and
a purpose-filled life. It is a well-known fact and true
from my experience and research that most people do
not accomplish their dreams. However, those people do
find a way to live a purpose, sometimes fulfill life with
far greater achievements than they dream. I suggest to
you that perhaps we have been focusing too much on
accomplishing dreams and not facilitating and encouraging
people to pursue a purpose-filled life. The great author Rick
Warren wrote an extraordinary book titled *The Purpose
Driven Life*. As a student and coach at Liberty University,
I remember when Rick Warren came to our campus and
did a weeklong study on a *Purpose Driven Life*. One of
the many things I remember about that week was *to be
purpose-driven* is to be driven by God's purposes, not our
own—what an amazing concept to think about. Often time
our dreams are a primary focus of some we achieve and
accomplish, many times leaving out God's purpose for the
dream. The key element is to understand there is a God's
purpose in accomplishing dreams.

Rick Warren further shares the idea behind being *Purpose Driven*, explaining,

> You are not an accident. Even before the universe was created, God had you in mind, and he planned you for his purposes. These purposes will extend far beyond the few years you will spend on earth. You were made to last forever! You must begin with God, your Creator, and his reasons for creating you. You were made by God and for God, and until you understand that life will never make sense. Being *Purpose-Driven* will help you understand why you are alive and God's amazing plan for you, both here and now and for eternity. The *purpose-driven* concept will take you on a spiritual journey that will transform your answer to life's most important question: What on earth am I here for? When that question is answered, you will be able to know God's purpose for creating you and will reduce your stress, focus your energy, simplify your decisions, give meaning to your life, and, most importantly, prepare you for your *purpose-driven* journey to eternity.

This is such a great perspective for us to learn and comprehend the depth of our purpose. So, you may ask yourself which one is more fulfilling? Which one is more satisfying? It is my understanding, and what I have come to know and experience is that I may not have accomplished my dream and goal of being a professional athlete; however, I have found a greater purpose-filled life. This gives me the adulation satisfying peace of knowing my life matter and count for something. I am humbled and blessed to know I have become so much more than my dream. Would playing in the NBA be a very satisfying accomplishment? Absolutely yes! Would the salary of an NBA player be satisfying as well? Absolutely yes! However, have you seen the statistics of NBA players once they finish playing basketball? Many end up broke and living an unfulfilled life, searching for significance beyond the court in unhealthy and unproductive things. I think we have done our kids a disservice by telling them about temporary moments and accomplishments of a dream instead of a long peaceful, grateful, satisfying purpose-filled life.

You see, living a purpose-filled life, in my opinion, comes from knowing the one who created you for the purpose. In my previous book, *They Called Me Coach*, I documented the difficulties and challenges that I face in finding my true peace, my true meaning of life. Yes, I have accomplished many things along the way that many people have not. I became a coach who experiences success, yet however, I still found myself not completely satisfied with who I was. Why is that? I believe it was because, at that time, I did not understand who Stephon Leary was and what he was meant to become. In fact, my point in the book is coaching chose me; I did not choose coaching. It gave me some direction to becoming something I never dreamed of, and I am grateful for the experience. But coaching is not my purpose; your profession is not your purpose. It only serves the purpose of an opportunity to truly live out your purpose, and that is to use that profession to tell people about a loving Savior in Jesus Christ and His desire to see every one of us accept Him so that we may enjoy heaven with Him.

Your profession is your platform to share the goodness of God in the land of the living. Jesus said, "He said to them, 'Go into all the world and preach the gospel to all creation. Whoever believes and is baptized will be saved, but whoever does not believe will be condemned'" (Mark15-16, NIV). I was a coach in a private Christian School and later coached at two Christian Universities, Liberty University and Palm Beach Atlantic University. Even when I was the head coach at a public university, I always shared the Word of God and tried to reach hearts and souls for the kingdom of God. However, I fell more in love with coaching and all the perks and joy I got from coaching. Now that I have learned through my many experiences, I am telling people, "You are more than what you see."

Because many of us grow up living our lives simply focusing on what we see and who everybody else is, instead of seeing what you can become beyond what you see. Especially when you pursue your purpose-driven life in Christ, I suggest to you that God sees us in a bigger light. He created us with greater purpose than what we understand, and it is not until we submit our lives to Him and seek Him through the difficult times, through our ups and downs, the broken and unfulfilled dreams, and beyond the generational curses that we discover and find the true meaning of who God created us to be and that true meaning leads us to a purpose-filled life.

Purpose in the Pain

One of my most common things to share with people is, there is pain in the purpose and purpose beyond the pain. Sometimes we get off track because we think the pain that we are experiencing is not in line with our purpose, yet I submit to you that it is because of the pain that we find our purpose. You have heard it often said many times,

"A diamond is not what it's worth until it experiences a polishing fire." Athletes do not become great athletes unless they train and abuse their bodies to maximize their ability to perform at the highest level. Life is the same way; we do not experience the greatness of who we are until we experience the pain of finding who we are. There is pain in the purpose. We have become so inundated with Disney fairytales that we have bought so much into dreams becoming true. Little girls dream of becoming queens and princesses, boys becoming kings and princes, that we forget not everyone can be in a position of a queen, king, or prince or princess, yet in your own life of understanding who you are, you can be a king or queen, you can be a prince or princess of God. It's all about knowing your purpose in God and dwelling in His presence. You are the pride of God's joy. You are God's king, and queen and I suggest to you that the purpose that He has for you is greater than what you see. Through all the pain, you can live a purpose-filled and accomplish life without accomplishing the fairytale dream. We must learn to check back into reality, and checking back into reality means we've got to go through something to be something, especially to accomplish something great. You can live a purpose-filled life through all the pain and disappointment. You can accomplish great things in your life; you do not have to sit around and be discouraged because your goals and your dreams did not happen the way that you thought they would. Often those dreams and those goals that we set are through the limited knowledge of what we know and what we see. God takes us through an experience of our own journey, our own life, that we began to see ourselves for more than what we have initially thought of ourselves. We start to let people define who we are and what we can be, and what we can do, instead of looking to our one and only true God, the Creator of heaven and earth.

We need to understand that there is a greater purpose than we know and think. And the greater purpose will lead you to a greater for filled life; this grading for filled life can only be accomplished through seeking, serving, and honoring Him, the one who created you for your purpose. Your dreams may not come true; most do not, furthermore the goals you set for yourself may not come true. Many goals and dreams depend on insinuating factors that play a role in why our dreams and goals do not come true. Those factors oftentimes are far outside of our control, yet, and still, there is a loving God through His grace, His mercy, and great love for us that continues to fulfill the purpose in which He created us. You are more than what you see; you do have a greater purpose than what you see and understand about yourself. Life journey will reveal that purpose; sometimes, it happens for others sooner than it may happen for you. It is taking me almost thirty years to realize my true purpose, and yes, I had some idea of what that purpose was, but I had some dreams and goals that I set for myself I thought I would accomplish or do that did not come true. Yet, I find myself still walking and fulfilling the purpose feel the life that God has set out for me, and God can do the same for you. It is on your journey to knowing and understanding who God is and what He has for you that you seek the giver of good gifts, not the gift. You have a greater purpose than what you see and understand about yourself beyond all your experiences and failures. The hurt, the pain, the fears, rejection, neglect, and your abuse, all of those things cannot keep you from living a purpose-filled life. God can take all of that and make something great out of you. There is greatness in you! You have to seek to discover all that God has for you and not be disappointed by the things that have happened that somehow make you think that life is over because you did not accomplish your dreams or your goals. There is more to life after those disappointments.

In his poem, "Harlem," Langston Hughes poses a question. "What happens to a dream deferred?" "Does it dry up like a raisin in the sun? Or fester like a sore—And then run?" Dreams are something God desires and wants for us; however, God's dreams are not so we can become famous or rich; it is so we can have a platform to share the goodness of our Savior and give Him the glory. God cares about our dreams. In fact, He places "God dreams" in each of our hearts. But, if I desire the dream more than God, *the giver of dreams*, I make the dream an idol. If I am honest, my desire to be a professional athlete was partly about wanting to feel a sense of significance, be accomplished, and be wealthy. God wanted me to find my worth in Him, not in the recognition and attention I could receive as a professional athlete. I also began to understand that He wanted to use the story of my journey and the pain from my past to bring hope and freedom to others. My life is not my own; there is a greater purpose for why we were created and why we have the talents and gifts we possess.

An Unexpected Journey to Fulfilling Your Purpose

Some people may have a very clear vision as to what eventually will do in their life; however, the journey to fulfilling that purpose may involve some unexpected twists and turns. Many of you may know the story of Joseph in the Bible. Joseph, in a dream, as a young boy, boasted to his family and brothers about how one day, they would bow down to him.

Then he had another dream, and he told it to his

brothers. "Listen," he said, "I had another dream, and this time the sun and moon and eleven stars were bowing down to me." When he told his father as well as his brothers, his father rebuked him and said, "What is this dream you had? Will your mother and I and your brothers actually come and bow down to the ground before you?" His brothers were jealous of him, but his father kept the matter in mind.

Genesis 37:9-11 (NIV)

Joseph did not know how it would happen, nor what it would take to get to that place where his brothers and family would come to him and bow down to him. His brothers, in envy and jealousy, stripped Joseph of the robe given to him by his father and threw him in a pit, and he was sold into slavery. I went through the areas of different trials in Joseph's life that begin with him being the favorite of his father, Jacob, who gave him a royal cloak. And because of this, his brothers despised Joseph and threw him into a pit, then sold him to men from Egypt and made him a worker. I bet Joseph never dreamed of being in the position he found himself in. Somehow when we have dreams, we only see the outcome. We never see the process of achieving or getting to the dream. I can only imagine what it might have been like for Joseph. God gave Joseph the ability to see visions and interpret dreams, and yet one would think if he could interpret dreams, how come he did not see what was coming his way in his own life? I think that is the trap that we all face in our lives when we reach or come to a place of unknown in our own life. It is always easy to help others and give advice to others. Perhaps, therefore, Joseph interprets others' dreams, so his gift was on display, but God desires for our talents and gifts to be used to glorify Him and not bring attention to ourselves. Maybe, therefore, we cannot possibly interpret our own dreams and visions, or else we would try and avoid the mistakes and challenges in our own path because we would lose sight of the gift giver, "God," and see ourselves for more than we ought.

He wants to use those mistakes and challenges to accomplish the dream. Paul says, "For by the grace given me I say to every one of you: Do not think of yourself more highly than you ought, but rather think of yourself with sober judgment, in accordance with the faith God has distributed to each of you" (Romans 12:3, NIV). If you can recall, in the Scriptures in Genesis, Joseph was falsely accused of sleeping with Potiphar's wife because he refused to sleep with her. So he was thrown into prison, but the scriptures said that God was with Joseph,

The Elevated Soul

And Joseph's master took him, and put him into the prison, a place where the king's prisoners were bound and he was there in the prison. But the Lord was with Joseph, and shewed him mercy, and gave him favor in the sight of the keeper of the prison.

Genesis 39:20-21 (ESV)

Imagine being falsely accused of such a terrible crime. Yet, just like God, the prison became a place for preparation for Joseph. The Scriptures tell us that while in prison, he found favor in the eyes of the guards. Sometimes in our lives, we find ourselves off track from what we ever would have imagined. It seems like all our hopes and dreams have died. But God always has a greater purpose no matter what happens to us in our life. Too many people focus on the dream being a place of destination and achievement instead of discovering the true purpose for why the talent was given to them. We somehow think if we fulfill the dream, we discover our purpose; however, in most cases, people fulfill the dream but still do not discover their true purpose. Like Joseph, there is life beyond our failures and disappointments. To conclude this wonderful story in the Scriptures, we discover that Joseph's gift of being a person who interprets dreams became the saving grace for all of Egypt.

Dreams vs. Purpose

When the king of Egypt had a dream that he was disturbed by, the only person to call upon was Joseph. Joseph was able to interpret the king's dream, which was a warning for a famine that would take over the land. And because of Joseph's demonstration of hard work as a servant and his faithfulness to God, he was elevated to be in command of preparation to prepare for the famine and help Egypt prosper during the famine. Do you see, even when things look desolate or hopeless, God is always working on our behalf? Yes, many of our dreams may not come to pass, but God has a greater purpose for you and for me. He desires to use your talents and gifts beyond whatever that dream was. Many people achieve certain dreams in their lives and still come to a place where they feel unfulfilled, and they need to find a greater purpose. A dream accomplished can be a place of achievement and destinations to celebrate to be proud of; however, there is life and purpose beyond the dreams. God cares about us, and He cares about our dreams. He cares enough that He is willing to redirect us away from what we think we want so that He can lead us into what He has for us.

There is a God dream for your life. It might be something you are already walking towards, or it could be something completely unexpected. I believe that as you hold your plans and dreams with open hands and trust Him with the process, He will lead you into the fullness of what He has in store for you. Sometimes the God dream requires sacrifice. As it turns out, God is more concerned with our character than our comfort level. We can let the hard things build our character or break it. We can sacrifice the dream for what is temporary, or we can persevere and allow perseverance to strengthen our character and build maturity in us in order that we accomplish a greater purpose in our life; God's purpose. Do not give up on your dreams, but understand it for what it is, a temporary moment in time. Do not let the pain or disappointment cause you to forfeit God's dreams for you, something far greater than you could imagine. Do not let quick fixes and momentary pleasures rob you of a greater calling. Do not give up, and do not give in. There is too much at stake. You are born with a purpose to achieve greatness beyond broken and shattered dreams.

There is freedom on the other end of your faithfulness. Both for you personally and for all the people who will be impacted by you fully living out your purpose! Through our faithfulness, God promises to redeem our dreams. This promise that God would redeem the dream, that He would restore me, gave me hope that the season I was in would not last forever. I know God to be a redeemer. I love the story of Joseph because it is an example of a dreamer who trusted God, even when it appeared that all of his dreams were shattered. He was betrayed by family, abandoned, enslaved, imprisoned, and forgotten. Through it all, God was with Joseph. Ultimately, his truth in God enabled him to rise above his circumstances and save his family and all of Egypt from famine. God used every single bit of Joseph's life and story for good! God redeemed the dream.

I wonder if Joseph was ever tempted to give up the dream. Instead, he stayed faithful throughout all his difficult seasons and circumstances, allowed God to use him, and kept dreaming. A nation was saved because of his faithfulness. God placed Joseph in a place where he could serve the purpose in which God gave him the dream.

I do not know what you are going through. I do not know what kind of trials you are enduring or the attacks of the God dreams for your life have suffered. But I do know this God is a redeemer. He is faithful. As you keep dreaming, keep trusting, keep persevering, God will redeem the dream!

SPIRITUAL EMOTIONAL AND MENTAL ANXIETY

Let me first say I don't have a PhD or master's degree in Psychology or a medical degree in mental health; however, I do have a Psychology degree in Human Service/Counseling from Liberty University, and I completed a few courses towards my master's degree in Counseling also. I also have experience and had the privilege and opportunity after college to work at Behavior Training and Research Center, as well as served as the Counselor for Faith West Academy High School students. While at Behavior Training Research Center, I was a house parent, and my role was to care for teenagers and young adults who were going through mental, emotional, and or behavioral issues, and they were placed in a home by parents or the Department of Mental Health.

Some could be assigned to the home because of juvenile criminal activity or runaways as well. I was not in the homes on the premises with clients who were handicapped or suffered from down syndrome and cerebral palsy. I was, however, involved with most other clients. I consider this stage of my life one of the most rewarding things I was able to do. It is interesting to me that this opportunity came along right after my dream of playing basketball professionally has just come to an end. Looking back as I write this book, I now believe God put me in a place where I had an opportunity to serve those in need. For me, this was perhaps my valley of "Dry Bones" experience. As a house parent at BTR, I worked four days on and four days off. At first, I thought to myself, *wow, I get four days off and only work four days, I'm in.* Little did I know what I was walking into. While BTR was a wonderful place and served its purpose for those who need a home away from their home for whatever reason, it was not long before you understood the depth of hurt these young people were dealing with. The outward expression and cry for help were immediately evident. My three other staff members in the house were responsible for three kids. There were twelve kids in the house altogether, and in times of overflow, we may get one or two extra kids. Boy, was I thrown into the fire, and like most, I said to myself, *What have I gotten myself into?* Through it all, I had the opportunity to learn a lot and observed the depth of mental, emotional anxiety, and physical limitations. So, while I do not possess the highest level of education that one may think I need to broach this subject, I surmise that my life experiences, among other things, add some value to the insight I want to share with you from my perspective, and hopefully give you some hope of a loving God who loves you and has a purpose for you regardless of your condition. The story of the valley of dry bones in the Scripture was not about the sadness of the valley but the condition of the people's hearts. So, God sends us sometimes to a desolate place to bring hope and love and share there is a God who loves them.

In the story, when Ezekiel passed through the valley of dry bones, in Ezekiel 37:2, he noticed two things: 1. That there were a lot of bones in the valley; 2. The bones were very dry. We find out later in Ezekiel 37:11 (KJV), "Then he said unto me, Son of man, these bones are the whole house of Israel: behold, they say, our bones are dried, and our hope is lost: we are cut off for our parts." The verse explains bones represented the spiritual condition of Israel during that time. The valley of dry bones that Ezekiel was led to was not a representation of nor a reflection of Ezekiel's present heart condition or his present season; rather, it was Israel's. In fact, the bones in the valley reflected Israel's spiritual state and season during that time. Sometimes, God will send you to someone else's dry valley in order to speak life. When God sends you into someone else's valley, as he did with Ezekiel, God wants to use you to speak life to a dry and defeated situation. During that time, their hope as a nation was dry and withered. As

109

people, they were emotionally drained, spiritually slain, and physically defeated.

It was not before long I realized my purpose for being at BTR. The beauty of being sent to BTR was that it was a refuge for people. The owner of the facility was a Christian and allowed us to pour into the hearts of these hurting people. I also realize why we worked four days on and four days off; by the time your shift was over, you were exhausted from dealing with all the many issues of twelve broken kids. As an employee and house-parent, we were also the teacher as well, so after waking the kids up and cooking them breakfast which one of us as staff members was responsible for, we then had to get them their meds, and off to school, we went. The school experience was another great challenge, many times resulting in fights and or emotional outbreaks. There were times when there was peace and quiet, and all of a sudden, a student would have an emotional outbreak, sometimes resulting in having to restrain the students to prevent harm to themselves and others. After school, we would always have inside or outside activities, and so that was fun, but it could also present some challenges. Once we got everyone fed and chores done, it was a time to relax. These became precious times where you could get to know your three kids one on one. Having the opportunity to speak to these kids' hearts became the most rewarding time. As much as I was trying to pour into these kids, they began to change me and my perspective.

Being a kid from a broken home who endured hardship, as well as some of my siblings, I felt like I had it hard, and to hear what many of these kids had endured, changed me. It was then that I began to see the opportunity for ministry. I realized why I was sent to BTR to learn to love the unlovable and be genuinely loved myself. Perhaps once again, reflecting back to the last chapter, my dream of playing professional basketball would have prevented me from this invaluable experience. There was a purpose for me working at BTR.

The Power of Caring

A group of us staff members had an idea about approaching the owner about implementing a behavior reward program. This program would allow for staffers to reward students with an off-campus visit to something fun and exciting. Introduce the kids to a new experience. The owner accepted our proposal, and so it began. We saw remarkable changes in the hearts and behavior of these kids. At the end of the day, these kids wanted to know someone cared enough to love them. The condition of their heart became hopeful; the sadness and discouragement turn to excitement. I personally witnessed life-changing miracles. I loved going to work, and after the four days were up, it was sad. Sometimes you return, and the state has removed kids, or they progressed well enough to go home. This reminds me of how God is to us. I know on the outside, the state of mind and emotions of a person look hopeless, but God heals the brokenhearted. Perhaps what we see and experience in many people's lives is a condition of their heart, and they have become hopeless, devastated, and have given up. By no means am I saying this for those who have been diagnosed with real physical, mental or emotional conditions, however, God's love for them is still available, and the condition of their heart can be changed.

I personally witnessed this while working at BTR. One of the students that I was responsible for in the house was a young man by the name of Jim (for the sake of non-disclosure, Jim was not his real name). We called him Big Jim. Big Jim was about five feet ten or five feet eleven but weighed over three hundred pounds. Big Jim was a challenge for us; however, when we started the behavior reward program, Big Jim found satisfaction and joy in spending time with me so much so that when I told Big Jim about the behavior reward program, I can still remember him saying to me while clapping and laughing "Okay,

okay, okay, I'm going to be good, I want to go to basketball games with you. I want to go see football with you. I want to go to church with you." And sure enough, the behavior of big Jim changed. Many times, I would sign Big Jim out and take him to church; I took him to see movies and took him to see football games. There was nothing like the joy on big Jim's face when we were away from BTR. This was a life-changing experience for me. I do not know where big Jim is today, but he changed my life. Big Jim taught me how to love. Big Jim taught me about giving hope to the hopeless. You see, Big Jim was one of our greatest challenges at BTR, and being the new guy, he was assigned to me.

In the beginning, I complained, I was not happy because Big Jim was one of our biggest challenges. For as sweet of a guy as he could be, he could be a living terror when he had an emotional outbreak or a mental breakdown. The explosion reminds me of a hulk-like explosion. While teaching Big Jim in school, Big Jim would get so frustrated he would start rocking, and when he started rocking, we all knew he was about to have an explosion. Big Jim's explosion came in the form of biting himself to the point where he would not let go, and we had to physically remove his arm from his mouth, which was a great challenge. Big Jim would suck his blood, and whoever

113

comes near him, he would spit it at you. It was a very, very challenging time when Big Jim had a breakdown. Big Jim's explosion could also result in banging his head up against the wall, turning tables over, and destroying everything within sight. This would result in two or three of us staffers having to restrain him and a possible injection to calm him down. That was the Big Jim I was assigned to, but the opposite side of big Jim was as soon as I arrived for work Big Jim ran up to me and gave me the biggest hug; he would almost squeeze the breath out of you. When I took Big Jim to see other people like my family members, and friends he would hug them the same way—he might also kiss you! Big Jim was full of love; it just took someone caring enough about him to bring that love out. Ladies and gentlemen, no matter what condition you find yourself in, and you have suppressed your desire to be loved, God wants to love on you. If we could just learn how much God loves us, it would change our state of mind and the condition of our hearts.

Scripture tells us he came to heal the brokenhearted and set the captive free.

> **The Spirit of the Lord God is upon me; because
> the Lord hath anointed me to preach good tidings
> unto the meek; he hath sent me to bind up the**

brokenhearted, to proclaim liberty to the captives, and the opening of the prison to them that are bound; To proclaim the acceptable year of the Lord, and the day of vengeance of our God; to comfort all that mourn.

Isaiah 61:1-2 (KJV)

If you feel hopeless in your situation, God wants to heal you and give you hope. If you feel unloved in your situation, God wants to love you and give you a big hug. I thought I was going to BTR to share what God had done or was doing in my life, and God used Big Jim to teach me lessons that nothing else could have taught me. I will forever be grateful for BTR and my relationship with Big Jim.

Anxiety and Its Meaning

As a disclaimer, I do not have the theological degree to know the depth of spiritual anxiety. However, what I have come to know and understand is that the enemy desires to destroy God's people with emotional, mental, and spiritual anxiety. David speaks of this anxiety and his failure, Paul speaks of his anxiety of not knowing, Jacob wrestled in the spirit all night with anxiety, and Jesus Himself had a bit of anxiety as He dwelled on the cross. Anxiety is a normal emotion, but it doesn't have to cause us fear, worry, depression, and insecurity. Let's quickly define what the word "anxiety" means.

Anxiety is an emotion characterized by an unpleasant state of inner turmoil, often accompanied by nervous behavior such as pacing back and forth, somatic complaints, and rumination. It includes subjectively unpleasant feelings of dread over anticipated events. Anxiety is also a feeling of uneasiness and worry, usually generalized and unfocused as an overreaction to a situation that is only subjectively seen as menacing. It is often accompanied by muscular tension, restlessness, being tired, and problems in concentration. Anxiety is closely related to fear, which is a response to a real or perceived immediate threat; anxiety involves the expectation of a future threat. People facing anxiety may withdraw from situations that have provoked anxiety in the past. Many people have anxiety when they are tired and feel like they're in a deficit, and fear comes upon them. I like that Scripture says that even young people get tired.

> Do you not know? Have you not heard? The Lord
> is the everlasting God, the Creator of the ends of
> the earth. He will not grow tired or weary, and
> his understanding no one can fathom. He gives

Spiritual, Emotional, and Mental Anxiety

strength to the weary and increases the power of the weak. Even youths grow tired and weary, and young men stumble and fall; but those who hope in the Lord will renew their strength. They will soar on wings like eagles; they will run and not grow weary; they will walk and not be faint.

Isaiah 40:28-31 (NIV)

When we get tired, if we at that moment could turn eyes to God and let Him renew our strength and not allow anxiety to overcome us. I liken us to babies when we get tired, we whine and complain, and sometimes in our lives, we whine and complain ourselves to anxiety and stress. Some parents describe this moment as their child is afraid they will miss out on something, so they fight their sleep. How much can we learn from a baby? Many of the solutions to help a baby during these times are to be held and comforted, to be fed, or to give them attention. Can this be a recipe for us when we face stressful times that cause us anxiety and fear? How about allowing God to feed you through His Word and His Spirit. I know for me, sometimes, the only place I can get perspective is when I get in the presence of God through reading His Word, listening to praise and worship, and just laying down sulking at that moment and pray. All of a sudden, my fear

117

is gone; my stress is reduced, and I feel filled. When we face times of trouble, do we live into the truth of God's constant care? Or do we turn to other sources for comfort? Do we pour out our hearts to Him, or do we choose instead to drown ourselves in sorrows in regret, self-pity, fear, or bitterness?

I have come to understand that anxiety, fear, and worry are a real thing. However, it has helped me understand how to fight the enemy who is wanting me to live in despair. If we can find joy in the toughest moments, we can find strength. Do you struggle with anxiety, stress, and fear? What do you do when these feelings come upon you? I have a very dear friend who is one of the godliest people I know, who loves God, loves people, does good to all men, and is one of the sweetest persons I know. However, spiritually, I believe the enemy attacks her with anxiety from time to time that usually is associated with the love or care for others and causes her to feel inferior and not herself. I also believe that this anxiety comes upon her when she is on the verge of a breakthrough or something good is about to happen. She allows this anxiety to ruin her day and feels insecure about all things. It is these types of situations I consider to be spiritual anxiety. Let us go a little bit deeper; in my own life, I experienced a lot of success on the outside in my coaching and training; however, many did not know or may not have known I had a lot of anxiety on the inside. Every single one of the opportunities that came my way, I had to face some anxiety in my life. Whether it was a new job, a new business, shifting to a new direction, financially and even socially, because I desired to make everyone happy, and when someone was disappointed in me, it affected my belief or my feelings about myself.

Anxiety causes us to feel insecure about who we are, what we are capable of, what we can or cannot control, and depressed about our situations and circumstances. That is the enemy of our soul who does not desire to see us be blessed, prosper, and be happy. God desires to comfort you during difficult times, especially when you are facing emotional anxiety. One of Jesus's finest hours is when He stood on a mountain and gave the sermon on the mountain called the "Beatitudes."

Now when Jesus saw the crowds, he went up on a mountainside and sat down. His disciples came to him, and he began to teach them. He said: "Blessed are the poor in spirit, for theirs is the kingdom of heaven. Blessed are those who mourn, for they will be comforted. Blessed are the meek, for they will inherit the earth. Blessed are those who hunger and thirst for righteousness, for they will be filled.

119

Blessed are the merciful, for they will be shown mercy. Blessed are the pure in heart, for they will see God. Blessed are the peacemakers, for they will be called children of God. Blessed are those who are persecuted because of righteousness, for theirs is the kingdom of heaven. "Blessed are you when people insult you, persecute you and falsely say all kinds of evil against you because of me. Rejoice and be glad, because great is your reward in heaven, for in the same way they persecuted the prophets who were before you.

Matthew 5:1-12 (NIV)

You see, these are attitudes of Christ that perhaps we should think about in our moments of anxiety, fear, and stress. The beauty of it is that Jesus didn't just say what we should do, but he also gave comfort in knowing the outcome. Sometimes our anxiety is because we do not see how we benefit from our situation. Release your anxiety, your fear, and stress to God. Let Him do a work in you! Sometimes we forget about God's ability to deliver us from our circumstances and our situations. Worrying, stress, and anxiety can kill us, which is what the enemy of your soul desires to do. Scriptures say, "Therefore do not worry about tomorrow, for tomorrow will worry about itself. Each day has enough trouble of its own" (Matthew 6:34, NIV).

I know, at times, it can be overwhelming when you are pursuing God's plan for your life. When God reveals His plan to you, it is usually beyond your current skill set or ability. It can also be beyond your level of education and outside of your financial budget. It will stretch you and challenge you to come out of your comfort zone and start becoming the person He desires for you to be. Sometimes this can leave us in a state of anxiety, fear, and insecurity, as we will tend to feel small compared to the *big* plan that God has shown us. Yes, it can seem overwhelming at times, but you must understand and know that it is not impossible. Nothing is impossible for Him. Believe in the one who can do all things. The bigger your problem, the bigger your challenge is, the bigger your God should be in your mind and heart. In these moments, when you face fear, anxiety, and stress, we must know that there is a God that is bigger than the things we face from day to day.

Confidence in God

The key to overcoming your insecurities is to start trusting in God's ability and not your feelings. When God called Gideon to raise up an army to defeat the enemy, Gideon was overwhelmed with feelings of insecurity, and I imagine anxiety and fear. He thought for sure how could he be the one to do such a great thing. He came up with every excuse possible that stemmed from his own insecurity. "I am too poor; I am too weak." Check out this conversation with God and tell me if you do not do this when you feel overwhelmed, and anxiety comes upon you.

> When the angel of the Lord appeared to Gideon, he said, "The Lord is with you, mighty warrior." "Pardon me, my lord," Gideon replied, "but if the Lord is with us, why has all this happened to us? Where are all his wonders that our ancestors told us about when they said, 'Did not the Lord bring us up out of Egypt?' But now the Lord has abandoned us and given us into the hand of Midian." The Lord turned to him and said, "Go in the strength you have and save Israel out of Midian's hand. Am I not sending you?" "Pardon me, my lord," Gideon replied, "but how can I save Israel? My clan is the weakest in Manasseh, and I am the least in my family." The Lord answered, "I will be with you, and you will strike down all the Midianites, leaving none alive." Gideon replied, "If now I have found favor in your eyes, give me a sign that it is really you talking to me.

> Judges 6:12-17 (NIV)

Spiritual, Emotional, and Mental Anxiety

How often in our lives do we allow anxiety, fear, and stress to come upon us because of our insecurities. We so often focus on what we do not have, what we can't do, what has happened to us that we doubt God and His ability to overcome whatever circumstances we may find ourselves in. Imagine living a life free of worry, stress, fear, and anxiety because we find peace, comfort, and trust in God. God did not leave Gideon in a state of insecurity, and He won't leave you there either. As you learn to trust in His Word and apply it to your life, you will begin to gain a level of confidence and courage that overrides any feelings of insecurity, fear, and anxiety. Remember that nothing great or extraordinary happens in your comfort zone. This means that you will have to break out of any insecure mindsets that you may have and start seeing yourself as God sees you. God sees you and a victor. He sees you as an overcomer. He sees you as a mighty person who is going to accomplish great things in life. I would like to make the suggestion that everyone has anxiety to a certain degree. We all face stress, anxiety and fears, and worries at some point in our lives.

It's not so much that stress, anxiety, fears, and worries come upon us; it's how we respond to those things that will dictate our ability to overcome them. First Peter 5:7 (NIV) says, "Cast all your anxiety upon me because I cared for you." I believe in these moments; we forget that there is a God that cares about us, and not only does He care about us, He cares about every situation and what is going on in our lives. However, when we face such anxiety and worry, we first look to try to resolve those things ourselves, and many times, those things are bigger and out of our control. In such a situation as physical illness, accidents, and incidents that happened that are beyond our control, and there is nothing we can do to resolve them within ourselves, we can always have a steadfast approach to trusting and knowing that God will take care of them. He is fully capable of delivering us from every single situation. Yes, I realize in some situations, people look to God, and lose a loved one, lose a job, experience financial despair, and does not discover their purpose and find success. However, God will use the pain in those situations for a greater purpose.

As I have learned and grown through many situations, I believe these are formative stages of God getting ready to do something big in you, and He is equipping you to be stronger to depend on Him more, to get guidance and direction from Him. These times serve as a preparation ground to building you up for the ministry and journey that lies ahead. God is always working on our behalf even when we do not see Him working, and that is the toughest part about being a Christian because that is where our faith lies. So, the question is not about whether there is a God or whether God can deliver you from your situation, but it often is, do we have the faith to believe and trust that God will deliver us from those situations? I have also come to understand that God did not have anything to do with how we grew up and the wrongful situations and environments and cultures that hindered our ability to experience success or even failure. But what we can do is grow through those experiences so that we develop a level of faith and trust in Him during those stages. So, we find ourselves often being tested at a later stage in life, and we question the very existence of God. Anxiety is, or can be used, as a tool of the enemy to discourage you and keep you from seeing God and His desire to use you and deliver you from whatever your situation is. I would like to remind you that as Moses delivered the Israelites out of Egypt, they came to the Red Sea, and they began to question God as if He did not deliver them before. I believe that way of thinking, that questioning, or that fear came from when they were enslaved in Egypt. Many times in our lives, we go through things that the enemy desires to use from our past to keep us from seeing our future. We get stuck in the present moment; we get stuck on seeing the obstacles that are in front of us instead of focusing on the one who can deliver us from those obstacles. The enemy is constantly lying to us, trying to convince us there is no hope. He says that life is too hard, that God is not good, and He is holding out on us. Our enemy wants to keep us confused and hidden. He wants us to doubt God and doubt ourselves—why? Because he is afraid of us. He is afraid of who we really are in Jesus and the plans God has for us. He wants to stunt our growth and stop us from being all we were made to be. God wants to reveal our true beauty as we change the world for His kingdom. When Job himself endures boils from top to bottom, even his wife tells him to "curse God and die" (Job 2:9). And yet, Job does not curse God, but he does ask why he was even born. He does not shake his fist and gives God a piece of his mind, but he questions the pain. We serve a God who is big enough that He can shoulder the why questions of life. We cannot, in our finite minds, understand or possibly even bear the answers to those questions during suffering, but God is still listening.

If you are enduring a hard thing today, do not be afraid to take your questions and your hurt to God. In His perfect timing, He will help you see His greater plan, and while you wrestle with "Why," He will continue to draw you near. The elevated soul of your life is reducing your stress, anxiety, fears, and trust and believe in God to deliver you and provide for you during every situation you face.

LIVING A LIFE OF GRATITUDE

One of the most powerful yet humbling positions we find ourselves in is a position of gratitude. Yet, I often wonder how many of us are truly grateful. Do we honestly understand what gratitude means? Could it be that the attitude of gratitude and the spirit of gratefulness is your key to a full life? Why should we give thanks or be grateful because Scripture says, "This is the will of God in Christ Jesus!" (1 Thessalonians 5:18, NKJV). Worry about nothing thanking Him for everything in every situation. Or could it be that the spirit of gratefulness elevates your soul and your ability to find peace in every situation? Maybe you have heard the saying, "Your attitude determines your altitude!" I believe this quote is absolutely true; in fact, I used this saying in my twenty-seven years of coaching, teaching, and training. However, I have learned that one of the greatest senses of attitude is gratitude. An attitude of gratitude of the heart is a pathway to experiencing God's peace—His blessings—and keeps you humble.

Attitude of Gratitude

Let us dive into an attitude of gratitude that keeps you humble. Scripture tells us, "Humble yourself in the sight of the Lord and He will lift you up" (James 4:10, NKJV). This is a picture-perfect example of an elevated soul. Imagine God lifting you up out of your despair, discouragement, or disappointments. Humility is a necessity to experiencing the greatness you were created to achieve. When you give thanks to God, you are giving Him credit and removing yourself or someone else from your success. You are saying it is not by your power, might, or wisdom; you're calling attention to Him, not to yourself. In fact, Scripture says, "So he said to me, 'This is the word of the Lord to Zerubbabel: 'Not by might nor by power, but by my Spirit,' says the Lord Almighty" (Zechariah 4:6, NIV).

It is the very spirit of God that propels us to see Him as our source of provision. This is very key because when we are able to acknowledge that it is by the spirit of God that we are grateful, it allows for Him to bless us even more. It also positions us to find ourselves grateful when things happen in every aspect of our lives because we see that it's not because we are so special that God blesses us; it is simply because He loves us and we give Him the honor and the glory for the things that He does and in our lives. Proud people do not thank God because it does not boost their ego, and they are quick to point out the person or persons for their success, which may increase favor in the eyes of others who may have shown them favor! They rather brag and call attention to themselves and others than lay the foundation of the favor of God. When we have a grateful heart and attitude, it is like laying a foundation on which God can build. Another way to look at it is making a deposit in God's bank that you may be able to withdraw from in your time of need. And you can only imagine what God's bank looks like. The blessings of God are never-ending.

It is not possible to be a sincere person of gratitude biblically and be proud at the same time. Thanksgiving keeps you humble, and the more you thank God, the humbler you become. The humbler you are, the more God is able to bless you in return. Far too many of us use gratitude as a way to say, "I deserve something in return," which defeats the person. It is not wise to show gratitude and expect something in return or want something in return. "Let gratitude be the pillow upon which you kneel to say your nightly prayer. And let faith be the bridge you build to overcome evil and welcome good"—Maya Angelou. I like the picture the great poet Maya Angelou gives us, "Let gratitude be the pillow." Humm, does this imply we find comfort and a soft place for our own head when we choose to allow gratitude to be our position of prayer? I believe in moments where we extend gratitude or choose to live a life of gratitude, we do find comfort and peace. The biggest issue with living a life of gratitude is pride.

Pride is trusting in your knowledge, skills, ability, and strength that you see no need for anyone else's help or acknowledge anyone else's help. Your pride will eventually destroy you. The greatest danger of pride is not seeing a need for a loving God and Savior and when that time comes where you need God, and you feel like He is not there, but the truth of the matter is you chase God away because your pride told Him you have no need of Him. Pride then begins to make you a self-righteous person who no longer is grateful and thankful. A life of gratitude is a life of humility which is the exact opposite of pride. I am reminded of the story of Job in the Scripture. Many people try to understand the life of Job because he suffered so much for what seems to be no reason. However, if you look at the Scriptures in Job 32:1 say that Job was righteous in his own eyes. A pretty dangerous place to be and live a life of gratitude. It also says in Job 32:2 that he justifies himself rather than God. Wow, so you see, it is dangerous for us to be prideful and self-righteous in our own eyes.

God then allows the storms of life to come in when we need something or someone greater than ourselves, we do not have the capacity to withstand the storm, and we become bitter in our lives instead of grateful. Gratitude is a choice you must choose to say thank you to others who serve you or give to you, but even greater than that, we must learn to serve rather than want to be served, and that is the true essence of a life of gratitude. Sometimes we can be misled by thinking gratitude is just being thankful for the good things that happen in our lives, and yet God sees it just the opposite. Scripture says in Matthew 20:27, let he who desires to be chief among you let him first serve. True gratitude seeks to help and serve others because we are overwhelmed and grateful for what we have that we want to make others' situation better.

Gratitude of Giving and Serving

One of the best ways to show gratitude is through serving others through giving. A great question we can ask ourselves each day we wake up is how can I serve and what can I give to someone else? What can we give to others that changes the state they are in and meets a need? I am not necessarily implying giving money, but more than that, we give of ourselves, our time, our knowledge, our wisdom, our helping hands, our testimony so that God gets the glory.

I love the story in the Scriptures about the beggar who sat at the gate called beautiful.

> **One day Peter and John were going up to the temple at the time of prayer—at three in the afternoon. Now a man who was lame from birth was being carried to the temple gate called Beautiful, where he was put every day to beg from those going into the temple courts. When he saw Peter and John about to enter, he asked them for money. Peter looked straight at him, as did John. Then Peter said, "Look at us!" So, the man gave them his attention, expecting to get something from them. Then Peter said, "Silver or gold I do not have, but what I do have I give you. In the name of Jesus Christ of Nazareth, walk."**

> **Acts 3:1-6 (NIV)**

What I love most about this story is when we find ourselves on the way or on our journey to doing what He calls us to do, He will place opportunities for us to give and be a blessing to someone else. Every day we wake up and head off to what we are supposed to be doing; God can and will use us. Even during this time of the pandemic, you may have Zoom calls, or simply by using your electronic

devices, we can always be a blessing to someone else. I
believe living a life of gratitude grants you opportunities
to be a blessing. It does not have to be about giving your
possessions or money. I believe the word "gratitude" is
being used and tossed around like it is a celebration that all
is well with you. However, the complexity in being grateful
or having gratitude is not about the good that happens; it is
also maintaining that peace and humility even when things
go bad for us. This is the more difficult aspect of gratitude.
Are we truly grateful when bad things happen? I encourage
you to be careful of such a trap that expresses joy and peace
only when things are going well.

Being Grateful through the Hard Times

Living a life of gratitude is the ability to be able to say,
"I'm grateful for the opportunity to have gone through what
I have so that I may learn and grow into the person that
God wants me to be through whatever difficulty comes our
way." The ability to say, "It is well with my soul." Scripture
says,

> **Do not be anxious about anything, but in every
> situation, by prayer and petition, with thanksgiving,
> present your requests to God. And the peace of God,
> which transcends all understanding, will guard**

133

The Elevated Soul

Philippians 4:6-7 (NIV)

Expressing gratitude for what you have and what you get to enjoy causes you to lose sight of serving and sharing with others. When we choose to express the times in our life when our cup is overflowing, we can forget about the purpose of the overflow and focus on ourselves. When life is good, and you're being blessed, God has a reason and purpose for blessing you, and that is giving back to Him to glorify His kingdom. Nothing wrong with rejoicing in the blessings you experience on your journey but be careful that your joy is only found in the good that happens. Scriptures say in 1 Thessalonians 5:16-18 (NIV), "Rejoice always, pray without ceasing, giving thanks in all circumstances; for this is God's will for you in Christ Jesus."

Being thankful in all things is the key. Again, I recall the story of Job amend; it was righteous in the eyes of the Lord, the Scripture tells us. However, he went through probably one of the most devastating times in his life and maybe even the lives of anyone that I know of. Because God had faith in Job and his commitment to the Lord, you're allowed for Job to be tested in a way that many of us would probably cringe to think of ever going through.

Living A Life of Gratitude

The scene of this encounter with Satan and God asking for permission to test Job is fascinating. Job lost everything, all his cattle, fields of wheat, wife, and children, and yet Scriptures tell us Job did not curse God or found any wrong. What is your attitude when you go through difficult situations? Does your attitude of gratitude change, and you find fault with God or with people? Gratitude is the ability to find peace and comfort no matter what happens. Sometimes we only find gratitude in the positive results of the trials; true gratitude thanks God for the trial as well. Learn to be a blessing and bless others and experience the greatness of what gratitude truly means. No matter what happens, you can find yourself in a state of contentment. *Gratitude brings contentment.*

It is said that gratitude makes what we have enough. If we are not grateful for what God has given us, getting more won't satisfy us either. Being thankful is the key to contentment. Godliness with contentment is great gain. For we brought nothing into the world, and neither can we carry anything out of it, but if we have food and clothing, we will be content with these (1 Timothy 6:6-8). Do you find yourself content with your situation or the things you have? There is nothing wrong with wanting and desiring more but being content says, "I'm okay with what I have" without complaining or being bitter. God blesses those who have a contented heart. The story of apostle Paul, while in prison, writes a compelling letter to the Church of Phillippi. An amazing attitude of gratitude considering he was stoned, beaten, and imprisoned and finds himself in chains.

> **I rejoiced greatly in the Lord that at last you renewed your concern for me. Indeed, you were concerned, but you had no opportunity to show it. I am not saying this because I am in need, for I have learned to be content whatever the circumstances. I know what it is to be in need, and I know what it is to have plenty. I have learned the secret of being content in any and every situation, whether well fed or hungry, whether living in plenty or in want.**

> **Philippians 4:6-7 (NIV)**

What jumps off the page at me is the joy and concern for others that Paul has while he seems to be the one in an uncompromising position. Being content with and without is the true position of gratitude. Being able to find joy and still be considerate of others can be a life-changing attitude of gratitude for all of us. How much does it really take to show gratitude towards others? Sometimes a simple smile, handshake, and hug can impact others. A simple *thank you* even when you don't feel like saying it can change other people's state of mind and open doors of their hearts for someone else to pour into. Gratitude can be the key that unlocks the doors of others' hearts and our own for God to pour into. Everyone has gone through something, especially as the world has faced the COVID-19 pandemic. I encourage all of us to step outside ourselves and find ways to show gratitude. Look for opportunities to show gratitude, and I guarantee you the lack in your own life will be filled.

Scriptures say give, and it shall be given onto you press down shaken together and running over (Luke 6:38). Can you imagine what running over would be like for everyone? A running over of joy, I'm running over of peace, I'm running over of love, running over of having instead of not having. What a world of difference we can make it shine and living a life of gratitude. Wouldn't it be nice to see joy on the faces of everyone? The last thing I would like to convey about gratitude is it puts us in a position where we do not become envious and jealous of others and keeps the enemy from trying to divide us and destroy us from within. Envy makes us want what someone else has. Gratitude makes us realize God has given us far more than we deserve, and there's enough for everyone. We can become a cheerleader for others rather than compare. A heart wholly grateful has no room left for envy. Scriptures tell us in Psalm 138:1 (NASB), "I will give

you thanks with all my heart." When your soul's purpose
of being thankful is on God with all your heart, it's hard to
think about someone else. The enemy wants us to compare
and think about what others have or have not. This is not
a new concept; it started from the beginning. Satan is so
deceptive! He whispers things like God isn't good, that
God withholds good from us, but his tactics are as old
as the beginning of time in the garden of Eden, where he
questioned Eve: "Did God really say, 'You must not eat
from any tree in the garden'?" When Eve responded only
the tree of good and evil was off-limits, Satan suggested
to Eve God was keeping good from them. "If you eat of
it, You will not certainly die. For God knows that when
you eat from it, your eyes will be opened, and you will
be like God, knowing good and evil" (Genesis 3). How
many times does the enemy try and deceive us into making
decisions where we get the credit and makes us think God
is not being fair? A heart of gratitude understands where
our source comes from and how good God is to us.

In a garden that was perfect, that produced abundantly
without work or weeding, where every single plant but *one*
had been given to Adam and Eve, Satan focused on what
they lacked or what they could have. True gratitude for God
and the abundance He gives protects us from caving to the
enemy's lies. The enemy is alive and well and longs to keep

us from experiencing the goodness of God. Psalm 84:11 helps us understand when we do what's right in the eyes of God; He blesses us—no good thing does the Lord withhold from those who walk upright. God is always looking down on us to find a faithful heart He can bless? Living a life of gratitude allows God to find your heart right before Him. It positions you to be blessed and experience an elevated soul in your life. Choose to live a life of gratitude, and don't let the pressures of life rob you of your gratitude for the things of God!

THE GREATEST OF LOVE

I want to try and broach this wonderful subject of love from various viewpoints. I think many of us have an idea of what love looks like to us or what love is supposed to be, but so often, I have experienced and have seen many people struggle to love and be loved. Why is it that we find ourselves so often feeling unloved? Is love a feeling? What is love? Throughout my years, I have read a lot of books, majored in psychology in college, and talked about love from the Greek methodology, biblical methods, and scholars' definitions of love. I wonder why there are so many different perspectives on this word called "Love." I Believe it is because when we fully grasp what love is and understand the depth of what love was meant to be, we will gain a greater understanding of our Creator, who loved us so much that He made us in the image of Himself. He sent His Son to die for us, He endures and fights for and with us, and He has prepared a place to dwell with Him in eternity. This might be too broad for many of us to understand, so I wanted to tackle this subject from my experience as a person who has two families—a white and a black family—a man who was divorced twice, a man who found love in his talent, a man who's coached thousands of kids in my twenty-eight years and had the pleasure of seeing love on display in many different families. I want to share what I have observed on the negative effects of love. I have grown to understand that love is complex. Yet, I also believe it is simple. So, where do we begin? Where can we begin to understand this beautiful word called love? Let's take it from the beginning. "So God created mankind in his own image, in the image of God he created them; male and female he created them"

I believe to understand love we need to understand who we are. As I have explained at the end of the chapters, when we lose sight of who we are or when we experienced trauma and pain from our past experiences, we no longer see ourselves the way we need to. To utterly understand what love is, we must understand who we are and where we come from. Remember in chapter one of this book, the greatest revelation for the young lion Simba was that his father spoke to him in a heavenly realm and told him, "Remember who you are." I have found that when I struggle with loving myself, receiving love, or feeling like I'm not capable of love, I realize I'm usually in a state of confusion, transition, setback, or experience something negative. Do you realize when things are going well for us, whether it is with our friends or family, our job, our profession, when we are experiencing success, it's easy to feel loved? However, the challenge with love is when we experience the negative effects of life, yet I believe the strength and the power of love is not just a feeling that we feel when things are going well for us. There are many people who have found the love of their life, and they can tell you the many tough days that they experience in that relationship, yet they find themselves still being in love.

Love is not necessarily when we feel good about ourselves and when things are going good; love is most prevalent during the time when we do not feel well. To understand that God created us in His own image is a very humbling feeling. How many of you see yourself in the image of God? Perhaps this is why you question yourself! I like to paint from time to time; I do not claim to be very good at it but, the Scripture made me think what a picture of Stephon Leary would look like if I created something in my own image. Would I draw a picture of love and beauty? What would I draw? God, in His infinite being and all His glory and majesty and grandeur, made us into His image. Scripture also tells us that God is love, so why is it that we don't feel loved or feel capable of loving? Certainly, if God is love and we were created in His own image, we have the ability to love and be loved. So how can we get to this place where we see ourselves the way God sees us?

Understanding God's Love

Let us take it a step further! If we understand where it all began, what's next? What's next about our understanding of this beautiful word, love? Scripture tells us in 1 Corinthians 13:13 (NIV), "And now these three remain: faith, hope, and love. But the greatest of these is love." Why is love considered the greatest of things? Could it be that because the greatest of love is so precious that it is the hardest to obtain? I don't know about you, but I find myself asking many questions about love. With all of the information that we can obtain, study, read, listen to pertaining to love, why do so many people not experience love? Could it be that many of us are so broken from our past experiences that we do not have the capacity to love or be loved? I want to share some insight that perhaps will free you to be all that God has called you to be and experience the greatness of His love and the love of others. First of all, let's get something straight; number 1) you are loved no matter what you've been through in your life, no matter what experiences you may have had, you are loved; 2) it is a lie of the enemy that he tells you you're not capable of being loved; 3) you can and will experience the greatest of love.

You Are Loved

The question is, how can we get to the point where we believe these things are true? You see, God used broken people to demonstrate His great love and purpose. You are not disqualified from experiencing the greatness of God. In fact, you are right where God wants you to be. "But God chose the foolish things of the world to shame the wise; God chose the weak things of the world to shame the strong" (1 Corinthians 1:27, NIV). So how do we move to a place from thinking we are not loved or capable of being loved? I love this song from Mercy Me called "Beautiful"; it says:

The days will come when you don't have the strength

When all you hear is "you're not worth anything"

Wondering if you ever could be loved

And if they truly saw your heart they'd see too much

You're beautiful, you're beautiful

You are meant for so much more than all of this

You're beautiful, you're beautiful

You are treasured, you are sacred, you are His

You're beautiful

And praying that you have the heart to find

Cause you are more that what is hurting you tonight

For all the lies you've held inside so long

And they are nothing in the shadow of the cross

You're beautiful, you're beautiful

You are meant for so much more than all of this

You're beautiful, you're beautiful

You are treasured, you are sacred, you are His

You're beautiful

Taking it a step further in knowing who you are is to realize we are God's offspring, meaning we have everything we need to experience the goodness and greatness of God if we abide in Him. What does it mean to abide in Him? It literally means to have our minds, hearts, souls, and spirits in complete unity with God. The things we think, the things that we do, are the things that He would think and do. And the only way to do that is to live our lives in and through Him. Through His Word, through His Spirit. In the natural sense of offspring, we can look at ourselves in the natural realm, and many of us look like our parents, and as you have kids, you see yourself in your kids. Not only do you see yourself in your kids, but they form mannerism, physical features, intellectual traits and inherit some of your personality, gifts, and talents. So the very word offspring of God is that we inherit all of the things of who God is, and a reflection of Him is in the way that we think, act, speak and conduct ourselves. We are God's offspring, and if we see ourselves the way He sees us ad act in a way that He would act, it would be impossible for us to find ourselves in a place of feeling unloved or feeling unworthy of love.

Throughout this book, no matter what the topic is, I am trying to help us all understand apart from Him, we are nothing and can do nothing. So, if you ever find yourself feeling like nothing, perhaps through the storms of life, trauma, and bad experiences in life, you have drifted apart from the very one that loves you and created you. Jesus describes this in a parable of growing fruit. Jesus says

> **I am the vine; you are the branches. If you remain in me and I in you, you will bear much fruit; apart from me you can do nothing. If you do not remain in me, you are like a branch that is thrown away and withers; such branches are picked up, thrown into the fire and burned. If you remain in me and my words remain in you, ask whatever you wish, and it will be done for you.**

> **John 15:5-7 (NIV)**

147

The Elevated Soul

If you are following along closely in this chapter, what I have communicated so far is helping you understand who you are in Christ (His creation). What you were created for (His purpose). When you were created (at the beginning in His image). Where you come from (His offspring). How God sees you (as beautiful), and how we can remain in His love. I believe in all of the books and studies of this amazing word called love, we have a lot of descriptions, and we tell people how we are to love; however, what I think is probably most important is to know who, what, when, where, and how, and why you are loved. So why does God loves you? Not only because you are His creation, but Jesus says,

> As the Father hath loved me, so have I loved you. Now remain in my love. If you keep my commands, you will remain in my love, just as I have kept my Father's commands and remain in His love. I have told you this so that my joy may be in you and that your joy may be complete. My command is this: Love each other as I have loved you. Greater love has no one than this: to lay down one's life for one's friends. This is my command: Love each other.

> John 15:9-13, 17 (NIV)

The Greatest of Love

What an unbelievable passage of Scripture Jesus communicates to His disciples, and He is still speaking that same passage of Scriptures to us. In these verses, we see the recipe on how and why God loves us and also how we can always feel loved.

God Is Love

The challenge then begins, since we know we can experience love ourselves and we can remain in love with God, we are in courage to love others. So, when you find yourself going through a period of time in your life, and you don't feel loved, for whatever reason, you can reflect back on your who, what, when, where, why, and how God loves us and compels us to keep His commandments and remain in love with Him so that our joy may be complete, and we can love others. If we all embrace this concept of love, we can begin to be a source of healing for ourselves and for others. As we dive more into this wonderful mystery of love, we realize that it all starts with knowing who we are in Christ, knowing you are loved, and how we are compelled to love others. Let us go deeper.

We must understand God has proven His love throughout the course of history and our time. We all know the most popular and famous verse in the Scripture

John 3:16 (KJV) "For God so loved the world that He gave His only begotten son that whosoever believe in Him shall not perish but have eternal life." I believe we experience a different life when we love the way God loves. Theologians, scholars, educators, and researchers all believe this love to be called *agape* love. If we understand our possibilities and capability of loving ourselves and loving others, it's because of the love that God has bestowed upon us. This could change the way we treat and love our friends, families, and even strangers. This agape love is defined as a Greco-Christian **term referring to unconditional love**, "The highest form of love, charity," and "the love of God for man and of man for God."

The greatest form of love is demonstrating the greatest sacrifice. God gave His only son! When we choose to love others, what sacrifice are we giving? The hardest thing for many of us to understand is until we are able to be in a position to feel loved by God, to love God, it becomes impossible to love others because we have nothing to give. And realizing giving is unconditional and does not expect anything in return. How are you loving yourself and others today? Do you live with the desire to want something in return? Are you loving others through sacrifice? This is why we find so many people are damaged by others because we don't know how to love properly, and even when we do know, do we have the capacity to do what it takes to show love? Many of us have experienced brokenness or a painful experience from neglect or rejection or abuse that we can't find within ourselves the capacity to love others, and we struggle with loving ourselves. We carry around the baggage of hurtful and painful experiences that prevents us from seeing and experiencing the love of God and the love of others. My goal in this chapter is to help you find love and understand you are never without love. God loves you no matter where you are, what you have done, or what has been done to you.

> **For I am convinced that neither death nor life, neither angels nor demons, neither the present nor the future, nor any powers, neither height nor depth, nor anything else in all creation will be able to separate us from the love of God that is in Christ Jesus our Lord.**
>
> **Romans 8:38-39 (NIV)**

Loving Others

Now because Jesus uses such a word as love with all your heart, love with all your soul, and with all your mind, we must look at other forms of love that scientists, researchers, and psychology have taught us. We have defined what agape love is, but many researchers and historians tell us about other forms of love. Some believe there are four core types of love *agape, storge, philia, and eros*. However, some people believe there are four more types of love like *ludus, mania, pragma and philautia*. Let's take a look at these:

1. Agape (the love of God god's love),

2. Eros (is the word for romantic, passionate love, suitably named after the Greek god of love and desire),

3. Philia (deep friendship, represents the love between friends, which can often be just as important as romantic love. "Philia can mean love between equals, love connected with the mind, and love between people who have shared hard times),

4. Ludus (playful love affectionate type of love." This might mean the love and excitement you feel when you have a crush on someone or when you're first getting to know them),

5. Pragma (longstanding love it's a love that has endured and matured over time and has meaning),

6. Philautia (love of the self refers to self-love or self-compassion, and the Greeks thought that loving yourself meant you had a wider capacity to love others),

7. Storge (family love refers to love between family members, like the love found between parents and children, between siblings, or between old friends that feel like family),

8. Mania (obsessive love, can also be a jealous and controlling kind of love).

All of these forms of love came from Greek methodology; one begs the question, does everyone believe in all of these aspects of love? We can see some form of love in all of these, but why describe love in so many forms, like it's a menu to choose from and chew on one at a time. I don't know about you, but I want to experience *true love* that embodies all of these characteristics. Here's what I have come to understand; we have failed to love others properly because we don't love like the Scriptures illustrate. Each one of these types of love is described from the scriptures as *one true love*. It even describes God's love as being a jealous love for us, describing it as a love that desires us for His own and dwells in His presence because our sinful nature causes us to wander away from God.

> **You shall not bow down to them or worship them;**
> **for I, the Lord your God, am a jealous God, punishing**
> **the children for the sin of the parents to the third**
> **and fourth generation of those who hate me, but**
> **showing love to a thousand generations of those**
> **who love me and keep my commandments.**

> **Exodus 20:5-6 (NIV)**

So, we go around hurting each other and say such things like, "I love you, but I don't like you," "I love you, but I'm not 'in love with you.'" We can't say I used to love you, "I love you, but I also love someone else," "I like being with you intimately, but I don't love you." Often this is a display of brokenness in someone's life that they don't either have the capacity or the capability of loving someone because of their own insecurities or hidden pain experiences. These sayings are a sad tale of someone who is choosing from the list and loving by one principle and not the others. Scriptures say, "And let us consider one another to provoke unto love and to good works"

Obviously, we can operate in these areas in our daily lives and establish boundaries in relationships like choosing *philia* "brotherly love" or friendship that is great, but when you choose to only use *eros* love and use someone, that's not love; Scripture says you are in lust, not love. Let's stop hurting each other and love each other truly. Let's give one another a shot, a chance to be whole and complete without harming each other. I understand in relationships, we discover that someone is not compatible, and you decide to go your separate ways or just be friends. But to subject someone to breaking their heart, or using them, or even abuse them for self-gratification needs to stop. If there is something revealed in you that needs healing, attention, or counseling, please take out the talk and do not hurt others or yourself.

God forbid that you would get to a place in your life that you do not love yourself enough; please do me a favor seek help. I promise you God loves you, your family loves you, and people love you. Do not let your hurt call you to make a decision to hurt yourself. You are loved! A relationship built on godly principles and *agape* love will be a relationship that has some form of all of this love that makes the relationship complete, and each person in the relationship is satisfied and fulfilled. That is what true love is all about. A relationship that is devoted to God and devoted to loving one another the way God desires for us to through friendship, passion, and intimacy, selflessness, growing and learning together committed to staying the course together honoring and glorifying God. Let us learn to love the way God desires for us to!

Who To Love

So, then what happens as we seek to love strangers and everyday people? A great question we can all ask ourselves is, does love have a color? Is love black, white, brown, or what is it? There is no such thing as describing love as a color restriction. It is sad that we have been blinded by history to believe that love pertains to the color of someone's sin. The sin of history, unfortunately, has blinded many into thinking it is better to love only with a race. Furthermore, it is sad that some people try to falsely use the Bible to make their point. Yet as I research the Scriptures, I have yet to find where any Scripture applies to how we are supposed to love others according to their skin color, race, ethnic group, or religion. In fact, we are told to love our neighbors and our brothers like we love ourselves. This clearly tells me to love whoever because Jesus was asked a great question, *"Who is my neighbor?"* when it comes to loving.

On one occasion an expert in the law stood up to test Jesus. "Teacher," he asked, "what must I do to inherit eternal life?" "What is written in the Law?"

he replied. "How do you read it?" He answered, "'Love the Lord your God with all your heart and with all your soul and with all your strength and with all your mind'; and, 'Love your neighbor as yourself.'" "You have answered correctly," Jesus replied. "Do this and you will live." But he wanted to justify himself, so he asked Jesus, "And who is my neighbor?" In reply Jesus said: "A man was going down from Jerusalem to Jericho, when he was attacked by robbers. They stripped him of his clothes, beat him and went away, leaving him half dead. A priest happened to be going down the same road, and when he saw the man, he passed by on the other side. So too, a Levite, when he came to the place and saw him, passed by on the other side. But a Samaritan, as he traveled, came where the man was; and when he saw him, he took pity on him. He went to him and bandaged his wounds, pouring on oil and wine. Then he put the man on his own donkey, brought him to an inn and took care of him. The next day he took out two denarii and gave them to the innkeeper. 'Look after him,' he said, 'and when I return, I will reimburse you for any extra expense you may have.' "Which of these three do you think was a neighbor to the man

The Elevated Soul

who fell into the hands of robbers?" The expert in the law replied, "The one who had mercy on him." Jesus told him, "Go and do likewise."

Luke 10:25-37 (NIV)

I love Jesus' answer to the question; it's quite funny when you think about it. It gives you one of those *duhhhhh* moments. I once heard a statement that I always challenged my players as it relates to "knowing" the scouting report and executing it; simply put, Jesus was saying this to the expert of the law "To do is to know as to know is to do." We know better, folks; let's do better and love everyone. We all deserve it. I love how Jesus used different people from different cultures to illustrate how to show love to a stranger. Knowledge is a powerful thing, and Scripture says we know that we all possess knowledge, but knowledge can be prideful, but love builds up. The man who thinks he knows something does not yet know as he should know, but a man who loves God is known by God (1 Corinthians 8:1-2). And the man who loves God learns to love beyond circumstances and the color of the skin because God is love.

Our pride will be the very thing that keeps us from experiencing the great things of God and enrich our own lives. Many of you may know my story, especially if you

158

read my first book, *They Call Me Coach.* I am a living
testament to this love as a young African American young
man; I ran into a few strangers myself that change the
course of my life forever. I encountered a white man, a
coach by the name of Dave Stallman. He was a man who
did not look at the color of my skin. However, he saw
my talent and my character or lack thereof. This man
who demonstrated love and extended his hand to me help
change the course of my life. Through him, I met one
of the greatest basketball players of all time, Pistol Pete
Maravich, who became a mentor and helped me understand
the truth about life and success. Coach Stallman also led
me to a life-changing moment as he introduced me to
more strangers, Dave and Lynne Johnson, and it was this
family, David, Lynne, Jacob, Jessica, Scott, and Billy,
who happened to be white adopted me into their family.
This miraculous event can only be described as an act of
God. You see, this coach Dave Stallman took me to a 5:00
a.m. prayer meeting in which the adults and parents of
children gathered together to pray for the families for the
children and for the day. It was at this prayer meeting that I
met—hey stranger—an angel in human form named Lynne
Johnson. Once the prayer meeting was concluded, Lynne
Johnson came up to me, having never seen me before, had
no idea why this young black kid of seventeen years old

would be at an adult prayer meeting, asked me, "So what are you doing here this morning?" This question would lead to an extraordinary change in the life of Stephon Leary. At that moment, Lynne Johnson told me that while we were praying, God told her to offer me a place to live. Not knowing my circumstances, not knowing anything about my current living situation, being a black kid growing up in inner-city Houston with a single mom and seven kids in a two-bedroom apartment, God spoke to her on my behalf. This, ladies and gentlemen, illustrates the kind of love that God has for us that He would speak to a stranger to change the course of your life and allow for you to experience the greatness of not only His love but of the love of those who love Him.

It was through this opportunity, this family love, and sacrifice, that an impoverished kid like me, from the inner-city who had no foundational structure, no educational structure, and no real direction that my life was changed. It is this kind of love beyond the color of my skin that we need more of today. With all of the happenings today in our country with social and racial unrest, each and every one of us can be a part of the solution. Perhaps to look beyond the color of someone's skin, look beyond others circumstances, and extend ourselves to love one another to build one another up, to empower one another, and to give each of us that hope we all crave and desire so that we give our next generation that same hope to achieve all their goals and dreams. Because of a white coach, a white family, this black man has now become a successful High School and College basketball coach, a trainer, business owner, motivational speaker, a best-selling author, and an inventor with a patent. Love changes things; acts of love will make a big difference in helping heal our nation. Jesus said in John 13:34-35 (NIV), "A new command I give you: Love one another. As I have loved you, so you must love one another. By this everyone will know that you are my disciples, if you love one another." It's important we as a people come alongside each other and show love and support. You are not alone in this world. "Be kind and compassionate to one another, forgiving each other, just as in Christ God forgave you" (Ephesians 4:32, NIV). For,

Two are better than one; because they have a good reward for their labour. For if they fall, the one will lift up his fellow: but woe to him that is alone when he falleth; for he hath not another to help him up. Again, if two lie together, then they have heat: but how can one be warm alone? And if one prevail against him, two shall withstand him; and a threefold cord is not quickly broken.

Ecclesiastes 4:9-12 (KJV)

The Elevated Soul

I courage each and every one of us to look for ways to show love for one another. And if you are in a position or predicament that you don't feel loved, I pray that you will find love in your Creator and allow Him to lead others in your path that will love you help you on your journey. Let us not allow everything that's going on around us or going on in us to keep us from expressing and showing love towards one another regardless of race, social and economic class, or religion. Love is the answer, and if we choose to live by the love that God has shown us and we show toward others, we will experience an elevated soul in our life.

> Love is patient, love is kind. It does not envy, it does not boast, it is not proud. It does not dishonor others, it is not self-seeking, it is not easily angered, it keeps no record of wrongs. Love does not delight in evil but rejoices with the truth. It always protects, always trusts, always hopes, always perseveres. Love never fails. But where there are prophecies, they will cease; where there are tongues, they will be stilled; where there is knowledge, it will pass away.

1 Corinthians 13:4-8 (NIV)

THE LIFE OF A TRUE CHAMPION

Let's look at the definition of *champion*; Merriam-Webster says a winner of first prize or first place in competition, or one who shows marked superiority.

The way a champion is described appears as if it is a positional truth; however, what I have learned and discovered is that living the life of a champion does not necessarily mean you finish first in competitions. As a former athlete who played several sports and won championships on several teams as a player and also won many championships as a coach in several sports, I would like to challenge your thoughts about "a champion."

When I was a kid, I can remember when two rival gangs or two people argued in class or lunch, and they used to say to each other, "Meet me after school," laughing out loud! For the remainder of the day, everyone would talk about the big fight after school or even on the bus. There were times I was afraid to ride the bus to and from home because of so many fights. But I love the concept of "Meet me after school" while it sounds terrifying, it sets the stage for your greatest achievement. That is the same stage that game day in sports gives us, the anticipation and thrill of knowing you get to compete against the best opponent to prove who you are and what you are capable of, and after every victory, you gain confidence in who you are.

We have to realize that it's our adversity that makes us a champion, the opponent, the challenge, the disease, the less fortunate situation, and the stage is set every day we wake up. We have a tremendous opportunity to be victorious in some way somehow. There is this slogan in sports where coaches tell our players to go out and "win the day!" Each practice, each class, every decision you must make win the day. You see, you have to develop a championship mentality before you can experience being a champion in life as well as sports. Let us take the life of David in the Bible, one of the most fascinating concepts of being a champion. In one fail swoop, David became the people's champion as well as a victorious champion. I submit to you that you are a champion; it is not just about the wins and losses in sports being a champion far exceeds an event. The event crowns you in one aspect but positions you in another aspect to live like a champion. David stumbled upon the greatest opportunity a person could face. But perhaps, from some people's perspective, it was the most fearful opportunity he could face. This is a clear picture of faith over fear. You see, his brothers and all the army were fearful of this "team" of people called the "Philistines," who also had the Michael Jordan of armies called Goliath. For those that are not familiar with this story, in 1 Samuel 17:1-51, a young shepherd boy named David, who was sent to deliver food to his brothers and the army to feed them while they were in this standoff, stare down against the mighty Philistine army and this giant called Goliath. I love this story because it encompasses so many aspects of life that we face every day and especially as athletes and competitors. This story takes place to prove who God was to him.

God will use your enemy as your footstool to demonstrate His purpose for your life; when you accomplish God's purpose for your life, you will look back and see a path of a champion. As a former coach, we won many championships, but they were simply moments in time. The life of a champion goes on, and the opportunities you will have to conquer and win from day to day will determine whether you have truly become a champion.

Let God Silence Your Doubters

You see, David was not as big as Goliath, nor did he have the weapons Goliath had, and *no one, I mean no one,* believed David was fit or capable to be in the position he found himself in to become a champion. Not even his own brothers, as it is stated in the Scripture:

> **When Eliab, David's oldest brother, heard him speaking with the men, he burned with anger at him and asked, "Why have you come down here? And with whom did you leave those few sheep in the wilderness? I know how conceited you are and how wicked your heart is; you came down only to watch the battle." "Now what have I done?" said David. "Can't I even speak?"**

> **1 Samuel 17:28-29 (NIV)**

Can you imagine playing on a team where your teammates discouraged you from wanting to go to battle with your opponents? I love this fascinating concept of young David, who had confidence and a belief in himself that exceeded all his brothers. I suggest to you that we're going to be a champion in life if we have a similar attitude to David by believing in ourselves, believe in our talent, and our ability to fulfill our purpose in what God has for us. David believed in himself because he believed in what God was doing in and through him, and not what he could do on his own? Look at this verse where David declares to Saul, the army, and his brothers why he felt so confident

and his ability to defeat Goliath. In 1 Samuel 17:34-37
(NIV), David described why he was so confident in his
ability to defeat Goliath he recalled to memory for things
that God has delivered him from before, and he uses this as
motivation to believe not only in his own ability to believe
that God will deliver him as He has done before. Check out
these verses in the Scripture:

> **But David said to Saul, "Your servant has been
> keeping his father's sheep. When a lion or a bear
> came and carried off a sheep from the flock, I went
> after it, struck it and rescued the sheep from its
> mouth. When it turned on me, I seized it by its hair,
> struck it and killed it. Your servant has killed both
> the lion and the bear; this uncircumcised Philistine
> will be like one of them, because he has defied the
> armies of the living God. The Lord who rescued me
> from the paw of the lion and the paw of the bear
> will rescue me from the hand of this Philistine.**

As a former player and coach, I love this attitude,
confidence, courage, and toughness David illustrated and
communicated to Saul. I submit to you, and there will be
times in your life that the people who are close to you,
those who've you pay higher respect to like your coach
or others in authority, may not believe in you, but a true

champion is one who not only believes in their own ability but believes in the God that created him. The God who will give him the ability to be a champion, to overcome whatever it is that they are faced with. You got to love the fact that Saul, being the king at the time, serves in the role in this situation as David's coach; how many of you have played for a coach who did not believe in you? How many of you work for a boss who did not believe in you? How many of you have grown up in a family where your parents did not believe in you? I bring good news to you today that despite those who do not believe in you, God has a purpose for you.

I believe you can look back over the years in your life and see small areas where God has come through for you, where God has delivered you, where God has sustained you, and if He did it, then He will do it again. No matter what the giant looks like in your life, no matter what the challenge is in your life, we serve a God who is the greatest of champions, and He will not fail you when you put Him first and choose to honor and glorify Him in your time of need. What excites me most about this passage of Scripture is David was not just against insurmountable odds and faced what looked like an unwinnable situation, but what excites me is he sees the moment of opportunity to allow God to use him in a situation where no one thought he

could win. I can't tell you how many times as a coach I
took teams to tournaments or scheduled opponents that
had a bigger name, and when we showed up, they were
bigger, they were more athletic, and my players or my team
would come to me and say "Coach, are you sure that's
who we supposed to play?" I also had parents who would
come up to me and say, "Coach are we playing that team
with all those big guys?" It's in these moments where we
realize that before we even give ourselves an opportunity to
achieve victory, we walk in defeat by what we see instead
of believing in who we are and what we are capable of. Not
only believing in what we are capable of but believing that
perhaps in this situation, God will allow for our talent to
shine forth.

I believe we have to get used to the idea that God likes
us going against giants and face with interminable hearts.
It's His opportunity to show up big for us, to declare you
as a champion, and by being a champion in that battle, you
give Him the glory so that others may believe in Him and
give Him glory. Being a true champion, you realize that
each battle you face that seems like you cannot overcome,
those are the times where God shows up and gives us a
victory. It is our faith in Him that gets us through, helps us
overcome, and makes us a true champion. Scripture tells us
that it is in our weakness He is made us strong. I am happy

to report to you that on many of those occasions when my teams were faced with giants of opponents, we were able to win by utilizing our skills and abilities. However, there were times where we did not win, and those times were because we did not believe; we allowed our fear to keep us from believing that we could be a champion on that day. The difference between faith and belief versus fear is one of the most challenging battles everyone faces today. When we walk in fear, we give fear the right to paralyze us, immobilize us from demonstrating our faith, our belief as skills, activities, and most of all, allow God to show us a favor and those moments. I want to take you a little deeper into the story of living life as a true champion.

You Are Enough You Do Not Need Someone Else's Armor

The next thing in the Scriptures that I noticed about David and his challenge with Goliath, Saul was okay with David going, but he tried to tell David that he needed his weapons, his protection, his defense mechanisms. But David rejected them, and he said to Saul, "I have no use of these. I've never used them before," laughing out loud—wow. I love that response! What an illustration of courage, of belief, of confidence in his own ability. Many times, we are faced in life where we are surrounded by people who don't believe in us, and they think that their skills, their talent, their ability, their way of doing things is what you need for you to be successful, and what you need for you to be a champion, and I submit to you today as I write to you that you are more than enough. You have all the things that God has given you to be a champion in this life. You have talent, you have skills, you have abilities; you are far more equipped than you probably know. The challenge in becoming a true champion is not winning battles or winning competitions, it is realizing that you are more than enough, and the talents and skills and abilities that you possess, God will use them when you're faced with the greatest giant in your life, so that you can one day overcome that giant and realize that you were created to be a champion. You were created with purpose! You were created to stand before Giants and declare the greatness of our God, not because of your talent, ability, and your skills, but because there is a God who loves us and has a plan for us. He desires to use us and give us victory over the battles we face. God will fight for you!

You see, battles are going to come at us in many forms, many different situations. It is not just about being a champion on the court on the field in the arenas; it's about being a champion in life. Your greatest opportunity to be a champion is staring at you right now today. No matter what your situation is, God will and can deliver you from it. Will you take your step in facing your giant and allow for God to show up big for you? I submit to you that I have learned over the course of these many years of being a coach and an athletic competitor in many sports, as a player that the many championships, but I have been privileged to be a part of never gave me the feeling of a true champion until I came to the place where I knew and understood what a true champion is. Being a champion and living your life like a champion does not mean you win sports championships; it means that you win in the game of life. You see, the greatest opponent you face in your life is "you." Can you get victory over your fears, your insecurities, your pains, your setbacks, your unfortunate situation, your disease, your sickness? Can you overcome those things by believing in a God that is bigger than the giant that you face in your life? I once heard someone say, "The greatest battle that we face is the '*in-a-me*' and not the enemy." If we realize that we are more than conquerors through him who we believe and then we are ourselves, we give God the greatest opportunity to help us become the champion in this game of life, and we get to live as a true champion and not live in defeat. You are more than enough! You are more than a conqueror! You are a victor and not a victim! You are a champion!

A Champion in Your Life

May I suggest to you a champion is not just about competition, the trophies, and winning the trophy, but a true champion is one who wins the battle of everyday life events of life. I would like to suggest that being a great dad, father, husband, and wife, mother, son, daughter, friend is being a champion. And ultimately, those who find their true purpose in this life and use it to serve the greater good are champions. I have come to learn that we wear the crown of champion in sports and competitions, but I see champions in everyday life. People who are conquering challenging things in their lives through personal growth, personal achievement, as well as professional and business are champions. The champion that I thought I was as a coach and a player has switched my thinking. I now believe the greatest championship is one who can celebrate his life and the challenges he or she conquers. "Enter through the narrow gate. For wide is the gate and broad is the road that leads to destruction, and many enter through it. But small is the gate and narrow the road that leads to life, and only a few find it" (Matthew 7:13-14, NIV).

Finding your true purpose in who God created you to be, overcoming the obstacles and the enemy of your soul to fulfill that purpose is a champion in life. In this wonderful book of *The Elevated Soul "you are more than what you see,"* I have tried to illustrate how we could become more than what we see even if we have had success or failure. As a coach and player, I celebrate my life with championships and rewards, but we are more than those things we have accomplished. As a coach and player of thirty-plus years of my life, I celebrate my life of conquering or achieving championships by wearing the rings and having a garage full of trophies, but most importantly beyond that life, the greatest achievement is celebrating the lives I have been blessed to have an impact on, and the crown I wear of being a child of God. Arriving at a place in life where I never thought young Stephon Leary would ever become an author or best-selling author, nor would I have ever thought I would become an inventor with a patent. You are a champion beyond the victories and achievements in sports. I would like to say there is a champion in you beyond the courts and field of athletic competition, and that champion understands there's a course of life to be run, and it's going to take courage, strength, and I believe confidence in the one who created you. Philippians 4:13 (NKJV) tells us, "I can do all things through Christ who strengthens me." You can do more than what you see, even if you have had some level of success. The champion in you has a life to conquer, a race to run in this competition of life. Will you become the champion that God has created you to be? Will you allow for Him to use you beyond the athletic fields in court of competition and fulfill a purpose greater than those levels of achievement? There is more to be done, and the podium is waiting on you to take your place in this life. Our society needs men and women, sons and daughters, to strive to be a champion in our ability to add to our society through love, kindness, hard work, teamwork, working together for greater calls, and most of all, sharing the good news of Jesus Christ who can save everyone from their sins and give them eternal life. That champion description tells us there is a crown in heaven that awaits you. Scripture tells us, "However, I consider my life worth nothing to me; my only aim is to finish the race and complete the task the Lord Jesus has given me—the task of testifying to the good news of God's grace" (Acts 20:24, NIV).

I love, love, love, sports, and I share in my book *They Call Me Coach*, sports saved my life, and to some degree, gave me life and a reason to live. However, it was God that used sports to truly save my life and set me on a path to fulfill my purpose in which He created me to be. If you find yourself at a point and a place in your life where perhaps you have lost many battles, you have lost many competitions, or you have won many battles, and won many competitions and were even crown champion, and you are still not fulfilled, I challenge you to go a little deeper into what God has in store for you. He has a greater purpose and plans beyond your wins and losses in life. The ultimate goal in our lives is to be found righteous before Him, so we may be crowned a champion by God. The world needs more champions for Christ. I was blessed and fortunate to earn a basketball scholarship and compete for Liberty University, and even return and coach at Liberty University, in which we won a championship. But the greatest thing about Liberty University was not my ability to be able to play and compete or coach; it is to be a part of an organization in which it tomorrow is building champions for Christ. As a young adult, I was challenged with understanding the concept of what being a champion for Christ was truly like. The late great Dr. Jerry Falwell, the founder of Liberty University, used to always tell us the importance of understanding what a champion of Christ was. It is someone that no matter what your path is in life or your profession, lives a life that is pleasing to God. Run the race that you may obtain the prize that is in Christ Jesus. This race that we run has a greater reward than any reward that we can have in heaven; the Scriptures tells us: "Now there is in store for me the crown of righteousness, which the Lord, the righteous Judge, will award to me on that day—and not only to me, but also to all who have longed for his appearing" (2 Timothy 4:8, NIV).

I believe that many of our most accomplished athletes get stuck in life because they're not thinking about discovering their purpose beyond their athletic ability. I've seen it often happen with businessmen as well. They climb the ladder of success so fast and accomplish great things, and when the transition of jobs happens, and you are being fired or laid off, they lose themselves. The fight in a champion to rise to the level of achieving something great requires a source of energy and strength that we sometimes forget when things happen in our life. That champion still lives within you! You are destined to be a champion and for greatness, if you choose to live the life that God has called you to live. We can all add value to this life. There are so many different capacities in which we can display a championship heart. The beauty of competitions is that there are individual races and team events; regardless of which one you see yourself as, you must be a star in your role in order for you or your team to be victorious. Never allow yourself to see yourself as a victim but always pursue victory. There is purpose in who you are. If you are a father, your children need to see the champion in you. If you are a mother, your children need to see the champion in you. If you are a husband, your wife needs to see the champion in you. If you are a wife, your husband needs to see the champion in you. If you are a child, do not look down on yourself because you are young; Scripture tells us that you are the example of the world. "Don't let anyone look down on you because you are young, but set an example for the believers in speech, in conduct, in love, in faith and in purity (1 Timothy 4:12, NIV).

There are people watching you; perhaps you don't realize the magnitude of your position in this world; not only are your parents and grandparents, aunts and uncles, sisters, and brothers watching you, they all need to see the champion in you. Never think that your life does not count. You are a champion! I find that many times we are chasing after the one thing that costs us in this place that we are running an alarm. As a former college and high school coach, I would sometimes get frustrated that we could do all the right things and play so well, and at the drop of a dime, certain players or individuals choose to get a script and because of not to perform at the level in which we were capable. It makes me wonder where you are in your life and your pursuit of being a champion for growth. Have you gotten off-script? Have you tried things your own way? And Proverbs 3:5-6 (NIV) says, "Trust in the Lord with all your heart and lean not to your own understanding in all your ways acknowledge Him and He will make your paths straight."

The Life of a True Champion

A straight path to achieving the life of a champion comes in trusting God, submitting and subjecting ourselves to obedience to living the life that He desires for us and not our own. Do you want to be a champion? It's a question that I asked my team often when we chose not to play the right way or do the right thing. Do you want to be a champion? If your answer is yes, then I would say let's go to work. That same training mindset, that same effort, and energy, confidence, courage, and boldness spirit of competitiveness that it took to be a champion in competition will be required in becoming a champion in the game of life. But when you get tired, don't grow weary; Jesus says in my weakness, you are made strong (2 Corinthians 12:9-11). You will have a difficult time; you will have challenges, the Scripture promises that. However, you are an overcomer; you are destined for greatness. There is a champion that lives in you, and it's up to you to strive to accomplish it. Proverbs 3:14 (KJV) says, "I press toward the mark of the high calling in Christ Jesus." I love the fact that this first says "press," I always think of it as being the heavyweight on a bench press that sometimes in life you just have to press it up off of you. Whatever you do, don't give up, and know that you can see a champion beyond what you see and have experienced. There is a champion in you! The elevated soul of your life knows that God created you with the purpose in mind that you can become a champion for Christ and one day receive your crown righteousness if you seek Him with your whole heart.

CROSSROADS

Reflecting on the year that was 2020, who would have ever thought as advance as technology is, and how quickly we are able to communicate and translate information, that we would face a life-changing, life-altering deadly pandemic like COVID-19, also known as the Coronavirus ? The Coronavirus pandemic has had an unprecedented, widespread impact on individuals and households across America, raising concerns about our ability to weather long-term health, financial harms, and employment, which has left many people wondering what to do next. Fortunately for some Americans, the impact of COVID-19 did not cost some people their jobs; however, it changed how they work and changed their daily and weekly routine. So ultimately, everyone was affected in some way or another. While billions of dollars have been appropriated by federal and state governments since the start of the Coronavirus outbreak, a series of polls by NPR, the Harvard T. H. Chan School of Public Health, and the Robert Wood Johnson Foundation found that a substantial share of households has not been protected from serious impacts of the pandemic across many areas of residents' lives.

"The Impact of Coronavirus " poll series offers a
national look at the problems emerging from the pandemic
relating to household finances, jobs, health care, housing,
transportation, caregiving, and mental health. "The Impact
of Coronavirus on Households, By Race/Ethnicity" explored
serious problems facing households in high-risk racial/ethnic
groups across the nation during the Coronavirus outbreak.
In particular, findings highlight the experiences of Latino,
Black, and Native American communities, who have all been
disproportionately impacted by COVID-19 with high rates
of cases, hospitalizations, and deaths. One in five households
in the United States (20 percent) reports household members
unable to get medical care for serious problems. A majority
unable to get care when needed (57 percent) reports negative
health consequences as a result. More than one in three
households that includes anyone with a disability reports
facing serious financial problems; many having trouble
affording utilities and food. More than one in three (36
percent) households with children face serious problems
keeping their children's education going, and among working
households, nearly one in five (18 percent) reports serious
problems getting childcare when adults need to work. About
one in three households with children (34 percent) either
do not have a high-speed internet connection at home or
report serious problems with their connection while doing

schoolwork or their jobs during the pandemic. About 43 percent of rural households report any adult household members have lost their jobs, been furloughed, or had wages or hours reduced since the start of the outbreak, with two-thirds of these households (66 percent) reporting serious financial problems. Further studies also show a significant impact on the psychological well-being of individuals and households in America. Depression and suicide are at an all-time high. So considering where we are and what has happened to us in this world, I would like to offer some comfort and insight.

First of all, God is no stranger to pandemics or outbreaks; He is fully prepared to help you in your time of need. Jesus promised in this life we would have troubles of *all kinds*. But He says, "Do not worry," He has overcome it all. Sure, this has changed life the way we know it and has affected us greatly. God is prepared to help you right where you are.

God is our refuge and strength, an ever-present help in trouble. Therefore, we will not fear, though the earth give way and the mountains fall into the heart of the sea, though its waters roar and foam and the mountains quake with their surging.

Psalm 46:1-3 (NIV)

I don't know about you, but it's comforting to know that God is an ever-present help as the Scripture outlines though the earth giveaway, isn't that interesting that God knows that things upon this Earth will not always be as it is? Yet, He tells us not to fear, and He promises to be a refuge and strength.

Keep Going Do Not Look Back

No question this has been a very difficult time for all of us, but the question remains; what will we do to respond to what's happening? In instances like this, I think we all find ourselves at a crossroad. Many times, we sit across the room as for options; however, once we begin to accept that the situation we face is what it is, the next thing that I believe is best for us is to make the determination that we can't go back. That is eliminating one of my choices. There is nothing to go back to; I know many people are saying they want life to go back as they knew it, but going back to something as you knew, will only bring more discomfort.

We must all accept the fact that it's time to *move on*. Yes, I know what you're thinking; move on to what? And that, I believe, is where many people have found themselves paralyzed by the moment that they feel incapable of moving forward. Perhaps it is because of fear, maybe it's comfortable where we were, or maybe it's because that's all we know, but I'm here to tell you many times in our lives as we get over the fear of moving on and embrace the challenge of moving forward, we discover a new level of strength, knowledge, understanding, and ability within us that will propel us to achieve an even better life and accomplish even more things. We have to accept the fact that we must inform and not go back. You can't go back! So now you wonder, should I go left or go right and discover something new, or should I keep going in the direction I was headed? This, my friends, is a crossroad. I find it ironic that this time and place in our lives is called "Cross-Road." Hummm, why is it so complexing at a time and place where we are unsure that we find ourselves at a cross? Isn't that interesting? Perhaps we are right where we need to be "*at the cross!*" Where we get our direction from the one who has a plan for you and has put you on a path to fulfill your purpose.

Follow Him

In a year where COVID hit, and I was forced to lay down my basketball and training program, something I had done for twenty-seven years, coaching and teaching the game of basketball through life's principles and providing teams for young people, I found myself at a crossroad.

The Elevated Soul

As I began to search and seek to find what it is that I'm supposed to do next, I found myself lost and confused. Coaching, teaching, and training in the game of basketball and sports, in general, was all I knew. It's why I wrote my first book, *They Call Me Coach*. The very nature of a crossroad, if we see it the way God sees it, is that we're actually right where we need to be at the cross. When you sit down and think about it, there was a time in our lives where we seem uncertain about the future or what the next step or next move was; that is what I described as a crossroad.

> **Then he called the crowd to him along with his disciples and said: "Whoever wants to be my disciple must deny themselves and take up their cross and follow me. For whoever wants to save their life will lose it, but whoever loses their life for me and for the gospel will save it. What good is it for someone to gain the whole world, yet forfeit their soul?**

> **Mark 8:34-36 (NIV)**

Here in the Scripture, Jesus describes our life as being a cross similar to that of which he died for us. He says whoever will take up the cross and deny themselves and follow Him will be saved. What has been your response to the pandemic? Have you panicked? Have you found yourself hopeless and, because of that, chosen to rely on the things of this world to help you through this crisis? The Scripture also says whoever will lose your life for Jesus' sake will save it, and He says something that we should always remember no matter if it's a pandemic or any crisis that comes in our lives and that is, "What profit a man to gain the whole world and lose his soul?" I believe that in times of crisis, especially one in the magnitude of what we have been going through, God is our refuge and strength. In Him, we can find peace, comfort, and direction! Scripture tells us:

Take delight in the Lord, and He will give you the desires of your heart. Commit your way to the Lord; trust in Him and He will do this: He will make your righteous reward shine like the dawn, your vindication like the noonday sun. Be still before the Lord and wait patiently for him; do not fret when people succeed in their ways, when they carry out their wicked schemes.

Psalm 37:4-7 (NIV)

This is one of my favorite verses when I come to a place of unknown or feel like I'm facing a crossroad. First, the Scripture says in verse 4, "Delight yourself in the Lord and He will give you the desires of your heart." God desires to meet those things that are in our hearts. He may go about accomplishing it a little differently, but it is good to know that He will give us the desires of our hearts. Next, it's two keywords, "Commit and Trust." We must choose to commit our ways to the Lord and trust Him to meet every need and desire. Then it says what I think is critical for us to know "God will reward and vindicate you"—what a tremendous blessing to know God will give us back what has been taken from us no matter if it's tangible or monetary or not. Are you ready to be vindicated? I know I am! Lastly, this passage of Scripture tells us to "Be still!" These two words can be found throughout the Scriptures implying God wants us to chill, hang tight, don't be overwhelmed. Relax and simply pray and watch God work. In my distress, one day, I had a revelation. On this particular day, I woke up and walked toward my kitchen, and the way my house is shaped, I could keep going straight or go to the right out my door or go to the left into my office or turn around and go back to my bed, *lol*. On this day, something occurred to me, and I said to myself, *I'm at a crossroads.* I was struggling with what to do with all this time I was having alone. Although, at this moment, I was trying to decide what to do about food or work, or relaxing. I felt like God gave me a picture of my life.

I think sometimes God allows for crossroads in our life to help us understand when we are lost; we need to see Him during our situation. So often, our first response is to figure out how to escape what we are going through, and once we realize we cannot escape it, we try and figure out how to make the best out of the situation. However, God has a purpose for everything that happens to us. Romans tell us for all things, He will work together for our good. On this particular day, I stood, and I thought to myself, *it doesn't matter what choice we make as long as we choose to follow God and know that He will be with us.* Often when we come to crossroads, the enemy of our souls wants to discourage us into thinking that we are in the middle of nowhere, or I say *"knowwhere,"* when in fact, God is saying that we are right where we need to be.

Have you ever traveled from one destination to another and found yourself thinking, where am I? But you know you are on the right road that leads to your destination. Sometimes on our journey to reaching the destination that God has for us, we will encounter challenges and perhaps come to a place of unfamiliarity, but as long as we trust in Him and stay on the path He has set for us, we will reach our destination.

Life Is About Choices

The pandemic has done major damage and clouded the vision of many people, and left them hopeless. Do not remain in that state; make a decision to stop and pray and ask God, what is it that He wants to do with your life beyond this pandemic? Sometimes God will just speak to us through our circumstances. As for me, on this particular day, I was hungry, so I could either keep going towards the kitchen and find something to eat, or I could go right out the door and go get something to eat, or I could go left and sit in my office and find some work to do, but that would not have resolved my hunger issues, and lastly if I turned around and went back to bed that definitely would not have resolved my hunger issue, and left me in the same position I started before. I learned a great lesson on this day. When we come to crossroads, it's not about how many choices we have; it's about eliminating options that do not fulfill or satisfy the challenge that we face.

I believe at every crossroad in our lives, there is something deeper inside of us that hunger for something, and we come to a crossroad to do simple addition and subtraction. You will find that things that you choose to do will either add value to the direction you need to go in your life or will subtract value from your life. I am not sure what your crossroad is at this time in your life; for me, it is about what's my next step into fulfilling the purpose that God has created before. Since I laid down my business, the only business and career I have ever known, I found myself in an uncertain time in my life.

Life is about choices, and it is up to us to choose what is in line with the purpose God has for us. Maybe God wants to take you to a new level and introduce you to another aspect of who you are. And this crossroad only represents your comfort level of wanting to go back and the fear of the unknown of moving forward. I began to wonder what God is calling me to do next in my life, and I was struggling with change. God always wants nothing but the best for you. So, no choice is wrong if you include Him in the decision through constant prayer and dwelling in His presence. There is just something different about God that He will choose to do in your life to continue to fulfill the purpose that He has for your life. The cost of going forward is the inability to go back to your past, and some of us are not ready to let go of the past.

Let Go and Move On

This is where we lose ourselves because what we know and what we are comfortable with weighs on us and pulls back, but the reality is you cannot go back—you just can't. Some things you want to go back to aren't even there anymore. Some people want the job they had that does not exist anymore. Many opportunities no longer exist. Certain relationships are no longer there. There was a reason why you left the place where you were in the first place; there is no reason for you to go back, but many of us are trying to go forward, holding on to what was in our past, and you are tired from carrying all that baggage. Let go of it! In order to find yourself and rediscover yourself and pursue the next step in your journey, you must be willing to let go of your past no matter how fearful, uncomfortable, or confusing life may be. Perhaps the greatest challenge in our lives is that ultimately, we are saying goodbye to the person that we know and have known, but this is the price and the cost of achieving new levels. When you come to crossroads, it is unfamiliar and presents a challenge of not knowing because what your talent and ability have brought you no longer can take you forward. Have you ever been to a nice hotel, and in order to get to the higher levels, you have to get off one elevator and get on another one? I guess sometimes in life, we come to the end of one road, and we have to get off and get back on another elevator to go up to the higher level. The pandemic and other circumstances or crises in our lives may serve as a stopping point or setback, but perhaps it's a setup for a step up.

Crossroads

In the first chapter of this book and the slogan behind the book *"you are more than what you see,"* I believe this; when we come to a crossroad, we have to understand we are more than what we see, and God sees more in us and is wanting to take us to a higher level. Getting stuck and having a hard time letting go of who you used to be, happens especially in the lives of athletes whose talent brought them to a place where all they knew about themselves was their ability to achieve and conquer things. However, when you reach a point where you can no longer do what you used to or live and achieve what your talent and ability used to do, you face a crossroad, and you have to know when to let go and move on. Knowing *when to let go and move on* will open your eyes and your mind to think about the power of perspective. Your perspective can motivate you or discourage you.

Relax. God's got you. Choose to make the decision to hold on to God's Word. Choose to hold on to His Promise. Find peace in the midst of your storm.

One day Jesus said to his disciples, "Let us go over to the other side of the lake." So they got into a boat and set out. As they sailed, he fell asleep. A squall came down on the lake, so that the boat was being swamped, and they were in great danger.

The disciples went and woke him, saying, "Master, Master, we're going to drown!" He got up and rebuked the wind and the raging waters; the storm subsided, and all was calm. "Where is your faith?" he asked his disciples. In fear and amazement, they asked one another, "Who is this? He commands even the winds and the water, and they obey him."

Luke 8:22-25 (NIV)

In this passage, we see the disciples were afraid because of the storm and the threat of them drowning, and in a panic, needed Jesus to calm the storm in their life, and He did. However, He said to them, "Oh ye of little faith!" Where is your faith today as it relates to your circumstances and situations, your crossroad? Our faith is what sustains us when we go through trials and tribulations in our lives. "And without faith it is impossible to please God, because anyone who comes to him must believe that he exists and that he rewards those who earnestly seek him" (Hebrews 11:6, NIV).

If you're familiar with the Scriptures, you may know of a famous story about a man named Noah. God saw how wickedness had become prevalent on the earth and decided to wipe humankind off the face of the Earth, but one righteous man among all the people of that time, Noah, found favor in God's eyes. With very specific instructions, God told Noah to build an ark for him and his family in preparation for a catastrophic flood that would destroy every living thing on Earth. God also instructed Noah to bring into the ark two of all living creatures, both male and female, and seven pairs of all the clean animals, along with every kind of food to be stored for the animals and his family while on the ark. Noah obeyed everything God commanded him to do. What does this story have to do about you and me? First of all, when there was a threat to wipe the earth clean, God found a righteous man in Noah and showed him favor. He chose to use Noah above everyone else. Scripture also tells us it was because of Noah's faith that God blessed Noah. "By faith Noah, when warned about things not yet seen, in holy fear built an ark to save his family. By his faith he condemned the world and became heir of the righteousness that is in keeping with faith" (Hebrews 11:6, NIV).

Pray and actively choose to rest in His peace. Let God fight your battle. Let God go before you. When it is time to war, God will teach you how to war. When it's time to war, He'll give you the strength and fortitude and weapons to fight. When it is time to fight, God will give you the wisdom and insight to conquer the enemy. When it is time to relax, choose to hold on to your peace and trust God; this battle belongs to Him. Choose to surrender to God and hold on to His Peace. Now I know and understand that when we come to some crossroads in our lives, there is an immediate need emotionally, physically, financially, or even spiritually. These desperate times that we feel when we're at the crossroads are still the same opportunity for us to look to God for immediate help. I believe that this is the elevated soul part of life; it is the ability to be able to trust God when we have to make tough decisions. Of course, there are certainly specific urgencies as it relates to financial deadlines, bills that need to be paid, and people need to eat and get medicine and treatment. I know this brings a level of fear and not faith; however, again, this is the elevated soul aspect of our lives. If we could just rise to the occasion and trust, hope, believe, and have faith that God will meet our needs according to His riches in glory in Christ Jesus. He says in His Word that He would never leave us nor forsake us, and at this moment, He will not leave you or forsake you. We must learn to overcome our fears and those negative thoughts that come into our minds that causes the crossroad of life to be more detrimental than what it's meant for. I believe we will always have crossroads in our lives because there will always be many factors that play a role in our journey to fulfilling God's purpose in our lives.

Of course, the one factor we know that there is an

enemy who does not want us to experience the greatness of God, nor His love, nor His provision. Scripture tells us in John 10:10 (KJV), as you find throughout this book, "The thief came to steal, to kill and destroy, but Jesus says I came that you may have life and have life more abundantly." We have to remember that God wants us to live in abundance if we will just see Him and trust Him. What's your crossroad today? Are you struggling with direction in your life? Are you struggling with self-worth? The crossroad that you are facing today is an opportunity for you to lay yourself down at the cross to seek God and allow Him to fulfill you in the way that He created you. Whether that be for your purpose, direction, healing, guidance, love, whatever it is, God wants to restore you.

BE FREE

The keywords to being free are surrender and submission. When you choose to surrender and submit your life to Christ, you experience a life like no other. When you make this choice, it's like you are giving your greatest gift to yourself in order that you may be fulfilled in return. You go through a process of releasing everything that has held you back and break free from the sin, shame, and bondage that you have experienced in your life. Why wouldn't anyone want to be free? Scriptures tell us that that □"His divine power has given us everything we need for a godly life through our knowledge of him who called us by his own glory and goodness" (2 Peter 1:3).

Prayer of Salvation

It's "His divine power" that gives us everything we need in this life to experience goodness. When you think about it, that is the greatest gift that God gives besides the gift of His only begotten Son, who died for us on the cross and rose again and forgave us of all our sins. John 3:16 (NIV) says, "For God so loved the world that he gave his one and only Son, that whoever believes in him shall not perish but have eternal life." Do you want to be free?

Have you ever taken the necessary steps to experience this freedom? I encourage you to do that even right now as you are reading this book. If the Spirit convicts you and compels you to take the time right now to set yourself free? God longs and desires for you to be free. Perhaps you're reading this book, and you have accepted Christ as your Savior, but you have gotten off track because of all of life's circumstances and situation that has brought you to a place of emptiness and bondage. You, too, can choose to be free again by simply submitting your life once again and allow for God to remove the bandage and terrible situation you may find yourself in. There is another great Scripture that says the law of the Spirit in Christ Jesus has set you free (Romans 8:2). There is no longer condemnation; you may be condemning yourself, or others may continue to condemn you, but through Christ, you can be set free.

"Therefore, there is now no condemnation for those who are in Christ Jesus, because through Christ Jesus the law of the Spirit who gives life has set you free from the law of sin and death" (Romans 1-2, KJV). If you want to be free, let's take a moment and settle this once and for all by simply praying this prayer with me "Lord Jesus, I recognize that I am a sinner, I recognize that you are God and God alone. Thank you, Lord, for sending your Son Jesus Christ to die on the cross for me that I may be set free. Please forgive me of my sins, come into my heart and make me a new creature that I may live a life that is pleasing unto you from this day forward in Jesus' name, amen."

I believe if you prayed this prayer that you are now a Christian, and the life of Christ does not stop; after the prayer, it starts committing yourself to live the way God created you to live. You no longer have to subject yourself to this world and find security in this world to find strength through substances in this world; remember the Scripture I shared earlier everything that you need is in Christ. Choose to read His Word, where you find knowledge, and instruction, and wisdom, understanding, and most of all, His principles that He desires for you to live out. I encourage you to find a mentor or a friend, a good church to plug yourself into; we all need accountability to our walk with Christ, and it is always better when we walk together with others who believe. You see, when you make this decision sometimes, you may feel reluctant to make a decision to walk away from the things that have brought you to a place of discouragement, disappointment, and unfulfilled. Let go of your past from this day forward and begin to live the greatest life you could ever experience, a life in Christ.

The apostle Paul was a man who was once considered

the most destructive person during his time. He was a
man that despised Christianity so much so that he killed,
tormented, and killed Christians. But one sunny day, Paul
came face-to-face with God, and he submitted his life to
Christ and became one of the greatest warriors for the
kingdom of God. Many of the chapters in the Bible came
from Paul and the life he lived. Paul had to forget his past
one day just like you and me. He's said in Philippians 3:13
(NIV), "Brothers and sisters, I do not consider myself yet to
have taken hold of it. But one thing I do: Forgetting what is
behind and straining toward what is ahead," from this day
forward press into the things that God has for you, do not
let your past hold you captive; be free and experience your
beautiful life in Christ.

I wanted to share with you my journey to finding
freedom. I recently wrote a book detailing my journey of
having been a coach, teacher, mentor, trainer, business
owner, entrepreneur, motivational speaker, an inventor
with a patent, and now a best-selling author. While this list
has many accomplishments, I found myself reflecting on
the life I lived. I'm excited about this chapter in this book
because it opens my eyes to the time where I submitted
and surrendered my life to Christ. Yet through my journey
in life, I had to come face-to-face with all of life's hurts,
pains, and disappointments on my journey. Writing this

book revealed so much I needed to let go and *forgive* in order to *live freely and enjoy* my life. I encourage you to take an inventory of what it would take for you to *be totally free*! Realizing that you need a savior is just the beginning; there is a process of releasing our past hurts and pain that has prevented us from living the life that God has for us. You are on a new journey now, a journey of fulfilling your purpose in who God created you to be. That journey sometimes will have challenges; Jesus said in this life, you will have trouble but take heed He has overcome them all. So, when you face those difficult times in your life, just know that you have an advocate and a friend in Jesus. Remember there was a time where you had nowhere to go, nowhere to hide, and you did not know where to turn, but now you have the greatest caregiver of them all, your Creator and your Savior Jesus Christ to lean on.

Overcoming Failure and Disappointment

Let's face it, for many of us, 2020 was a very difficult year in some way or fashion. For many, it's been a pile-on of what we were already going through or what we were trying to overcome. Perhaps in the midst of the greatest challenges, we can rise to greatness ourselves. As you look throughout the Scriptures and even in everyday life, many of our greatest achievers and most assessed people have endured and persevered through a life of failure and disappointment. As a former teacher of history, I love many of our historians, but perhaps none greater than the story of Abraham Lincoln. History tells us Abraham Lincoln overcame a lot of setbacks and hardships in his life. Some of which were devastating defeat in politics, failure, and heartbreaks, yet he became one of our greatest presidents. That is why still today in Washington, there is a Lincoln Memorial, and he sits on mount Rushmore. He lived a life that left a legacy for all of us to learn from. Below you will find a list of the many things that a historical writer once outlined about the many challenges Abraham Lincoln faced.

Lincoln was born into abject poverty in a one-room log cabin on Feb. 12, 1809, in the waning days of the Thomas Jefferson administration. Yet, he managed to rise to power, becoming the sixteenth president of the United States. Lincoln had no formal education. In fact, he even dropped out of grade school. His father, Thomas Lincoln, wanted him to become a farmer and frontiersman. Lincoln refused because he disliked the hard labor associated with frontier life, despite being strong and athletic and standing six feet four.

Be Free

This strained relations between father and son. Mostly self-taught, Lincoln was an avid reader, having read and reread, most notably, the Bible, the works of William Shakespeare, and Aesop's Fables. A self-educated lawyer, Lincoln eventually earned his law license in 1839 and went into private practice in Springfield, IL. At the age of twenty-three, Lincoln bought a general store in New Salem, IL, in 1832. The business wasn't successful, and he went bankrupt; it took years for him to pay off his debts. It was good for history that he did not prosper as a shopkeeper; this failure pushed him on toward other goals.

He lost his first love, Ann Rutledge, when she died in 1835 of typhoid fever. Lincoln suffered what is sometimes called a *nervous breakdown*. In fact, he suffered from depressive tendencies throughout his life. Lincoln ran for the US Senate and lost twice. He also ran for the US House of Representatives and lost twice before finally getting elected in 1846. The failures deepened his resolve.

In 1842, Lincoln married Mary Todd. Together, they had four sons: Robert, Edward, Willie, and Tad. The era was not kind to children. Edward died when he was three, and Willie died at the age of eleven. Tad died at age eighteen, six years after his father's death.

The Elevated Soul

In 1860, Lincoln was elected president by less than 40 percent of the popular vote. He gave his inaugural address knowing that Army sharpshooters were guarding him against any Confederate sympathizers. He was heavily criticized by both Democrats and Republicans—his own party—while in office and was despised by half the nation. His presidency further polarized the American South on the issue of slavery and states' rights, resulting in many southern states seceding from the Union and the beginning of the Civil War, the bloodiest war in American history.

Still, he worked tirelessly to pass the Thirteenth Amendment to the US Constitution, which formally outlawed slavery throughout the nation. After the South surrendered, putting an end to the Civil War and reuniting the Union, Lincoln died at the hands of an assassin named John Wilkes Booth on April 14, 1865, at the Ford's Theatre in Washington, DC.

Yet despite all of Lincoln's shortcomings and all of his failures, so many people have been inspired by him. To this day, Lincoln is considered by scholars, historians, and the general public to be one of the greatest presidents in American history. With the exception of Jesus Christ, no historical figure has been written about as much as Lincoln. He is the subject of more than 18,000 books and counting.

Be Free

The Lincoln Memorial and Mount Rushmore pay tribute to him.

Lincoln will go down as one of the greatest presidents in the annals of history. He epitomizes the American dream: He came from nothing to eventually becoming the president of the United States. Despite his personal demons, despite everything that was thrown at him—and these were significant traumas—Lincoln managed to soldier on. Such resilience and such strength of character are truly awe-inspiring.

Ron Carley

What an unbelievable display of strength and character. Although Lincoln was faced with many challenges, failures, disappointments, and setbacks, he found strength in what many believe to be his relationship with God. Lincoln was a man of noble character. So we are faced with a pandemic, and many are faced with other significant challenges. How will you respond? The Scriptures tell us not by might, nor by power but by my spirit, says the Lord (Zechariah 4:6). Be free and lean on the Spirit of God to lead you and guide you to overcome whatever is holding you back. Be Free! Unfortunately, many people have allowed negative responses to penetrate their hearts and mind. Don't quit, don't give up for greater is He that is in you than He that is in the world (1 John 4:4).

"Ye are of God, little children, and have overcome them: because greater is he that is in you, than he that is in the world" (1 John 4:4, KJV). I believe the most difficult emotion to overcome and be free is "unresolved anger." When we respond in anger and bitterness, we open the door for so many life issues that bind us in our hearts, minds, and spirits. Whether intentional or unintentional, hurt is the most devastating thing each of us faces, and how we choose to respond will allow us to be free or live in bondage. Scriptures say, "Refrain from anger and turn from wrath; do not fret—it leads only to evil" (Psalm 37:8, NIV).All throughout Scripture, if you do a study on anger, it tells us how it leads to poor decisions, lack of understanding, rage, wrath, and all manner of evil thing.

You must guard your heart against allowing the pain of your journey in this life to make you angry. Ultimately what we discover is that most people start with anger toward someone or something, and eventually, they become angry at God for allowing things to happen. This is a technique and tool of the enemy to get you to be angry at the one who created you for greatness and created you to do great things, and yet we find ourselves angry at Him, and therefore, we live in bondage; no longer free. I can remember as a young boy desiring to be a professional basketball player when I got the news that I needed knee surgery; I found myself angry at God. In my recollection, this is the first time in my life that I became angry at God. I can remember this day as if it was yesterday. Going to school at Liberty University in Lynchburg, Virginia, we had many hills and mountains around us, and so the night before I was to have surgery, I found the highest point on a mountain, and I yelled at Godwin for the first time in anger, "why are you doing this to me?" I was hurt, I felt hopeless, I felt like my life was over because it appeared to me that my dream of playing professional basketball had come to an end.

This anger nearly cost me my future. I can remember walking down that mountain in my head, saying to myself, *Why even try to live this life of Christ?* I was so discouraged that at that moment, I told myself, *I'm just going to enjoy my life.* Do you see people what anger does? It rises up within us and causes us to do more damage to ourselves than we do to anyone else. The consequences of anger slave us and keep us in bondage until we choose to come to a place of recognition that God is not the source of the problem; He is the solution for a problem. Scripture tells us that everything God does is good, and no good thing does he withhold from his children (Psalm 84:11). It is a trick of the enemy of our soul to cause us to live in anger, and with that anger, we make many bad decisions. Some of us make life's most devastating decisions that rob us of a great future. However, God is still available to forgive us of our sin to free us from the bondage of sin, dust us off and use us for his glory. Do not allow anger to control you and rob you of some of life's most precious moments—be free!

Choose to resolve any anger that you may feel toward someone or something. We all have endured hurt from something or someone. Yet, in some ways, "unresolved anger" can be the easiest to overcome. You can simply make up your mind *once and for all* to cancel the debt of someone or something that has been done to you. You decide and declare, "You don't owe me anymore." That is what God does for us! A powerful releasing of hurt emotions and anger can free you to be everything God created you to be. The remedy for anger is *forgiveness*! The root of anger is the perception that something has been taken from you, or something is owed you, or something or someone is unfair. *Forgiveness* will allow you to see that person or thing differently and clear the path for you to live freely and enjoy your life! There are seeds of *greatness* inside you; get rid of the weeds that are choking your seeds

from growing, flourishing, and blooming into whatever
God has for you. Be Free! Here are some action steps for
you you to consider to become free. Ask God to help you in
this process:

(1) Search your heart and identify who you're angry
with, and forgive them. (2) Determine what they owe you
or took from you and cancel that debt. (3) Ask yourself
what was unfair about what happened to you and release
it to God (4) Ask God to give you the ability to forgive all
the wrong that has happened and forgive yourself (5) Don't
allow the anger to build up again, let go and let God deal
with it. Go *live* and be *free*!

Always be mindful, "According as his divine power
God has given unto all of us things that pertain unto life
and godliness, through the knowledge of him that hath
called us to glory and virtue" (2 Peter 1:3, KJV). When you
surrender to Christ, He gives you the power to surrender
and submit to His Word. It is not by your own good works
or deeds that you are saved. It is through Jesus Christ
that you are set free and delivered from the bondages and
strongholds of sin. He gives you the power and stamina
to obey His Word. It is through Jesus Christ that you are

reconciled back to God. It is through Jesus Christ that your appetite for the past is broken. You are free in Christ. When you receive Christ in your life, the Word of God becomes alive, active, and operative in your life. When you are in Christ, you are set free. The power of sin no longer has a grip on you and does not have the authority to rule in any area of your life unless you choose to respond through negative emotions like anger.

When you are in Christ, you have the choice to live free in Him. Choose life. Choose freedom. Surrender to Christ and be free! The elevated soul of your life is your ability to be free from all of life's hurt, pains, value, setback, challenges, and break free from the bondage which has held you captive. Commit to living your life through Christ and experience the freedom that He gives you to enjoy the abundance of Christ through His Spirit. Be free!

UNDERSTANDING OUR FIVE SENSES

I'm so excited to be sharing a topic with you that I have become enamored and fascinated with; our senses. As I was writing about "you are more than what you see," I began to realize that perhaps seeing is believing, but what happens when we do not see? And what can be done about it? Maybe just maybe, God intended to use those other senses to cause us to see. I believe that to be true. God created man with five senses so we can have communication with our minds, hearts, and souls. These senses give us the ability to interpret things and formulate a response or reaction. I'm amazed and astonished with God's creation of our body and the role our senses play. I want to share with you some information to maybe help you process why perhaps certain things happen or have happened. I believe we have allowed ourselves to function less than what we're capable of because we don't use our senses in the way God intended.

I chose to write a book with the model or caption "you are more than what you see." Obviously, seeing comes from sight, which is one of our senses, so it's only fitting to dive into the other senses and discover the purpose in which God created them. Have you ever thought you might only be living 20 percent of who you were created to be? Or perhaps 40 percent, 60 percent, or 80 percent? Therefore, causing us to perform at a lower level? What if we were able to function at 100 percent? What would that look like? Is it possible that we can function at 100 percent? Obviously, we know that there are people who become blind and cannot see, and people will become deaf and cannot hear. Living in a time of COVID-19, we have also discovered that some people have experienced the inability to smell and taste. Sometimes these inabilities are communicated as handicaps, but could it mean that people are not handicapped but yet over-capped? Many scientists believe that when one area of our census is deficient, another area is multiplied. I don't know about you, but I found this concept to be very fascinating. It causes me to wonder just what God thought when He created us and gave us five senses. So, let's dive into it and take a look at what we can reveal and discover on how we can elevate our soul through our senses.

The Five Senses

Sight: here's a great verse that helps us understand the power of seeing. "The eye is the lamp of the body. If your eyes are healthy, your whole body will be full of light" (Matthew 6:22, NIV). Love this verse which places a lot of emphasis on how important seeing is; some people say, "The eyes are the window to the soul." Isn't it interesting that people look into eyes and make perceptions? Perhaps there's some truth to what they are saying. We all know we get weary eyes and sleepy eyes, but what about the eyes that fill the whole body with light! Hummm? Do I see the world through God's eyes and the path He wants me to follow? Are there any "blind spots" in my vision that I need to remove? Look to the hills which cometh my help; my help comes from the Lord. The maker of heaven and earth.

Taste: "Taste and see that the Lord is good; blessed is the one who takes refuge in him" (Psalm 34:8, NIV). Here we see the analogy of taste as it refers to the goodness of God and the comfort He provides. So isn't it funny that in life, we see food as a comforting thing? But most important, the sense of taste also provides sight. I find this fascinating because I know I love to taste the things I see. Have you ever wondered why the food on television or billboards looks so good that it makes you want to go and buy it? Later we will discuss how this can help us in our lives. How can I add flavor to my life today? Where am I getting my nourishment, my flavor for life, from today?

Feel: "She came up behind him and touched the edge

of his cloak, and immediately her bleeding stopped. 'Who touched me?' Jesus asked. When they all denied it, Peter said, 'Master, the people are crowding and pressing against you'" (Luke 8:44-45, NIV). There are many illustrations of touch; however, I like to think of touch as a change agent. We see in this Scripture, one touch from God is all we need for healing. To go a step further, in our everyday life, the touch of someone's hand, a hug, or kiss, can change their state of mind. Touch is a powerful element when used for good. Jesus healed the sick, raised the dead, and caused the blind to see simply by touching them. How are you using your power to touch others for good? How can I show God's love by being His hands to the needy, poor, or helpless or to those whom I love?

Hear: I'm going to use use a couple of verses for hearing because there's a dichotomy between listening and hearing. "Whoever has ears, let them hear" (Matthew 11:15, NIV). "Listen and hear my voice; pay attention and hear what I say" (Isaiah 28:23, NIV). You see, there are many times we are conflicted with listening to something and hearing something. So what's the difference? Merriam-Webster defines hearing as the "process, function, or power of perceiving sound; specifically: the special sense by which noises and tones are received as stimuli." Listening, on the other hand, means "to pay attention to sound; to hear something with thoughtful attention; and to give consideration."

Have you ever found yourself deciphering between the specific sound that you hear when you hear music playing? Or perhaps the intensive sound of the tone or levels raised in the voice of your mom or dad calling you, and you know when they are serious or not? That is the difference between hearing and listening. Hearing goes a little deeper into the specifics of the sound. Sometimes you hear people say, "man, I love the drums," or the trumpet, or the saxophone, and that song they are hearing, that music and not nearly just listening to it. This is a very interesting concept and applies to our relationships with one another and, most of all, a relationship with God. Do we truly listen or hear and act obediently to what God has in store for us? Do my words sound pleasing to others? Am I speaking with love? Am I listening for God's voice?

Smell: "For we are to God the pleasing aroma of Christ among those who are being saved and those who are perishing" (2 Corinthians 2:15, NIV). Can you believe that God sees us as a sweet-smelling aroma? How many times in your life have you been in a place where you have felt like life stinks, and you stink? Not to imagine or forget there are times where we are actually stanky, laughing out loud; that's the word that we use growing up. When you really stink, you stank, *lol.* To know that there is not a place we can get to analyze, and God doesn't think of us as a sweet aroma of Christ is a wonderful thing to know. No matter where you are, no matter what you've done, you smell good to God. I wonder what type of aroma are you around your friends, and your family, at work, out, and about? What type of aroma are we to other people? Our attitude and time can communicate love and care for others? Am I extravagant in my love and care for others that it leaves a lingering sweet aroma?

Now that you see all the senses and the possibility of how they can add value to our lives, how can we begin to operate with all of our senses to maximizing our life and experience the elevated soul in our life? In chapter one of this book, we took a deep dive into the psych factor and understanding the importance of knowing we are more than what we see, and you can see from the Scriptures that the eyes are the window to our soul. But one bags to question what happens when we can't see? As I shared in chapter one, Helen Keller says, "The only thing worse than being

blind is having sight but cannot see," a powerful illustration
of someone who may have the eyes to see but is blinded
by perhaps life shortcomings, disappointment, insecurity,

pain, and failure. They are blinded by not having a vision
for their lives, and yet that vision can be found in the one
who gave you sight and created you with a purpose. Helen
Keller also said, "The best and most beautiful things in
the world cannot be seen or even touched; they must be
felt with heart." When I came across this quote, I had to
stop and read it over and over again. I ask myself, how can
someone blind know such a thing? This is a person who
could not see that makes the statement that the best and
most beautiful things we cannot see and, guess what? I
agree.

What a magnificent way to look at our relationship with
God. You see, to live a life of Christ requires faith, a faith
beyond what we cannot see. In fact, the Scripture tells us in
Hebrews 11:1 (NIV), "Now faith is confidence in what we
hope for and assurance about what we do not see." What
a concept! I always thought to myself how the description
of something that I see, that a blind person can't see, they
described it as beautiful. I believe what Helen Keller was
describing to us was something she could feel in her heart
but could not see with her eyes. I think it's fascinating

that as we look deeper into the meaning of our senses, we discover how they all are tied together. And when we operate in one versus the other or choose to not operate and one or the other, we are shortchanging our lives. The beautiful thing is God gives an increase to the area that seems to be a decrease or deficiency. My grandmother, Opal Berard, in her youthful age of ninety-four, is losing her sight, and when I went to visit with her, she was sitting in the chair still so wise and eloquent, watching sports like basketball and football with the family and able to interpret what was going on and having a conversation with us, as if she could see—truly a sight to behold. But at this moment, I realize Grandma was over there knitting, and I asked, what are you making? She replied I'm making dishcloths, and your mother uses them on the business farm. She went on to say the ladies on the farm were running short of the dishcloths, so grandma said, "I told them I would make some more." She also said, "I can't really see what I'm doing, so they have little holes in them, but your mom, Lynne Johnson, told me those are just little holes of Opals love." Wowwww! What a beautiful, beautiful person, how sweet and loving she is? She also said would you like one? And I replied, "of course I would; why would I not want a dishcloth from grandma to always remember her bye" and so it happened I have one of grandma's towels. But this touched me deeper than just receiving a dishcloth. I left my parents' house where my grandma is living, thinking how in the world was she doing that, laughing out loud?

I began to think as I was writing this book about our senses, how Grandma had an elevated level of hearing, feeling, and touch that she was able to do something that I can't even possibly think about doing, and yet I can see. The faith we possess without seeing, tasting, touching, or smelling can come from hearing. Scriptures say in Romans 10:27 (KJV), "Faith cometh by hearing and hearing by the word of God." So, we see that there is an interconnection of our senses as they give us divine insight into the things of God and insight into our lives. Think about when you were a child, and you were told to not touch the stove because it was hot, to not touch the food on the plate because it was hot, and, in our ignorance—not using our senses of hearing—we would touch and get burned. Clearly, obedience comes from hearing when your touch sense doesn't have the awareness yet. Also, at that moment, we are denying our sense of sight. Oftentimes when things are hot, there is a level of steam coming from it, but we don't look to see before we touch. Most often, at this moment and other times in our lives, we are presented with the opportunity to use our senses. I would imagine the smell of the food is so good that we ignore our other senses. I

believe sometimes we are presented with an opportunity
and things in our lives that seem so good for us that we
ignore our senses and make bad choices that eventually
cost other opportunities and, most of all, experiencing
the blessed and prosperous life that God desires for us. I
believe this happens often enough that causes us to make
bad decisions and ultimately affect our lives in a negative
way because of the consequences we did not think about
when we chose to ignore our senses.

I know you can remember the many times your parents
or someone may have told you not to do something, and
you ignored the sound of their voices and did it anyway,
and it cost you. Perhaps someone told you something
about smelling gas and not to go near it, and unfortunately,
a blaze of fire burns here. I can think of many things
that happened to us when we ignore a certain aspect of
our senses, and those consequences are a result of our
disobedience. I believe the senses that God gave us were to
give us intuitive insight into making the best decisions in
our lives. I guess it could be said that our senses were given
to us so that we may become wise. Wisdom is the key to
obedience, and obedience is the key to righteousness, and
righteousness is the key to living a fulfilled life. Matthew
6:33 (NIV) says, "Seek The first the kingdom of God and
all of his righteousness and all these things shall be added

onto you." The life of an elevated soul, through our senses, comes from obedience seeking the kingdom of God and all His righteousness. Using a sense of smell, touch, taste, hearing, and seeing the impact the world in which God has the same. There are principles that are associated with the census that gives us the ability to live the life that God has called us to. When we choose not to use one of the other, our percentage drops in terms of the level of potential we have in Christ. The two most powerful parts of our body are our mind and our heart, and if you think about it, every time there is an opportunity to use our senses, they send signals to our mind and our heart to respond. When we deny using our senses, we are also not allowing our mind and our heart to function at their maximum capacity. In fact, what happens to us when we deny using our senses to make good decisions is that it causes an overreaction of mind and heart, which becomes worry, fear, anxiety, causing our bodily function to be thrown completely off physically, spiritually, emotionally, and metabolically. Using our senses in a positive and godly way can save us a headache and heartache. Our senses were given to us for our well-being, and when we abuse or neglect one or the other, it throws us off.

I believe we find complete peace and strength when our senses are operating as one. Let us not deny one of our senses used them all to honor and glorify God to impact the world in which He has placed us. When we choose to see things the way God sees them all of our senses are at work. God said in Genesis, He looked at what He created and said it is good! Scriptures also say in Psalm, "I remain confident of this: I will see the goodness of the Lord in the land of the living" (Psalm 27:13, NIV). "And walk in love, as Christ also hath loved us, and hath given himself for us an offering and a sacrifice to God for a sweet-smelling savor" (Ephesians 5:2, KJV).

"How sweet are thy words unto my taste! [yea, sweeter] than honey to my mouth!" (Psalm 119:103, NIV). "My sheep know my voice of God He who has ears let him hear" (John 10:27, NIV). "But God said, 'You shall not eat of the fruit of the tree that is in the midst of the garden, neither shall you touch it, lest you die'" (Genesis 3:3, NIV). If we touch others in kindness, but our words are the destructive noise, what does that say about how Jesus is working in our lives? I can bring the fragrance of the love of Jesus, but will it be canceled out by a bitter attitude or taste that I leave in someone's mouth? Serving and knowing God and choosing to live a life pleasing to Him involves using all our senses; He created them and intended for us to use them in his service. Don't take them for granted! Engaging God with all five senses can be a valuable tool in our praise, worship, and in our service to others! The key to living an elevated soul in our life is to be able to operate in all of our senses so that they function together as one.

We learn that seeing has everything to do with taste, taste has everything to do with smell, hearing has veering with what we see and touch, and each of these gives us a feeling that allows us to function in a spirit that honors God. Imagine the most loving, peaceful moment in your life. This may depend on you being single or married, but I know for me, the most powerful state of being I have ever been in is when I wake up in the morning after a nice clean shower and a nice breakfast that smells so good, and I have my praise and worship music on, and I feel the presence of God, and I eat my tasty breakfast, and it is filling. I always leave this time feeling love, peace, strength, and courage powerful that I'm ready for whatever comes my way. I wonder if we can make every day a day like this. A day where I feel the presence of God, I hear the sound of the music that glorifies Him, I taste and I see the goodness of God in my life, and because I just showered, I smell good, lol, and so does the aroma in the air. Our senses elevate our souls to living the life that God created for us!

FORGIVENESS

This is probably the most significant of all the elevated soul aspects of our lives—forgiveness! Over the course of my life, so many good things happened, but when trials and tribulations, setbacks, difficulty, trauma, and brokenness occurred, I didn't realize where that pain and insecurity were coming from. Oftentimes there is an injured place of forgiveness that is festering inside of us. There are three important aspects of forgiveness we need to understand; 1. God loves you and will forgive you for whatever you have done in your life, no matter how bad you or someone else may think it is. He will forgive you if you just ask. 2. We must forgive ourselves for all the bad choices we have made 3. We must find it in ourselves to forgive others, no matter what they have done to us. Whatever it is that you have experienced in your life, God is calling you and longing to forgive you. You must be able to see yourself the way God sees you. He longs to forgive you and bless you; you just have to receive it. Perhaps the most difficult thing is to forgive yourself. The self-inflicted wounds we punish ourselves with keeps us in a place of despair, and that's where self-doubt, depression, and a spirit of unworthiness hovers over you. Another difficult aspect of forgiveness is forgiving someone else for what harm and hurt they may have caused you. This could be the very thing that is keeping you from experiencing your best life and discovering a greater purpose. I have once heard it said that forgiveness is like glue. When we hold on to things that someone else did to us, we think we're going to show them or respond in anger, frustration, and whatever it is that we say or do bounces off them and sticks on you. You carry all of that inside of you until you get to a place in your life where you become aware of it, and now you're ready to take action. You can simply decide that you are willing to deal with it and ask God to give you the strength and ability to do so. Scriptures tell us, "For the eyes of the Lord run to and fro throughout the whole earth, to shew himself strong in the behalf of them whose heart is perfect toward him. Herein thou hast done foolishly: therefore, from henceforth thou shalt have wars"

I want to take you back to the movie *The Lion King,* in chapter one of this book, "you are more than what you see," I told you a story about Simba when he looked in the water closer he saw his father's reflection within himself and his father Mufasa appeared to him and said "Simba, you must go take your place in the circle of life," and Simba said, "No I can't, you don't know what I have done, I can't go back because of my past." His father then

responded, "Remember who you are; you are *my son,
the one true king*—remember who you are." I think it is
important in our lives that we remember the day we were
born, and for those who have become a Christian in their
life, it is important that you remember who you are as a
Christian; we all are God's children. There are some things
that hold us accountable to who we become based on our
relationships, especially our relationship with God our
Father. In the movie, when Simba had to face his father
Mufasa, I believe it is very similar to us having to come
face-to-face with a God that loves us. He cares for us, and
He has a purpose for us, and yet we have forgotten who we
are. We have been led and controlled by our past painful
experiences that we have forgotten who we are. Along that
journey carrying all that pain, disappointment, hurt, and
yes, sometimes it could be a load to carry, God wants you
to remember who you are.

It is my opinion as you remember who you are that
you must forgive those who have hurt you. I know it could
be hard to forgive, but it is the essential key to releasing
you and freeing you from the bondage that you carry on
the inside of you. Sometimes we think of life as things
happening to us and not happening for us. If we change
our perspective and see that God will use every experience
to accomplish the purpose for which He created you, and

there is nothing, absolutely nothing, that can keep you from the purpose in which God created you. But you must release the pain inside of you by forgiving yourself, forgiving others that may have hurt you, releasing the anger and frustration of past failure. There is such an amazing experience that happens when we allow God to cleanse us to free us from our brokenness. I reflect back on the song that the great Christian writer Kirk Franklin wrote, "Imagine Me." In the song, he illustrates the powerful state or position of imagining me being free—what a powerful, powerful place to be. The song says:

> This song is dedicated to people like me.
>
> Those that struggle with insecurities, acceptance
>   and even self-esteem.
> You've never felt good enough, you've never felt
>   pretty enough
> But imagine God whispering in your ear letting you
>   know that everything that has happened is
>   now...
> ...gone, gone, it's gone, all gone
> (It's all gone, every sin)
> Gone, gone, it's gone, all gone

Forgiveness

(Every mistake, every failure, it's all gone)

Gone, gone, it's gone, all gone

(Depression, gone, by faith, it's gone)

Gone, gone, it's gone, all gone

(Low self-esteem, Hallelujah, it's gone, it's all gone)

Gone, gone, it's gone, all gone

(It's gone, all my scars, all my pain)

Gone, gone, it's gone, all gone

(It's in the past, it's yesterday, it's all gone, ah)

Gone, gone, it's gone, all gone

(I can't believe it's gone)

(Gone, what your mother did, what your father did,
    Hallelujah)

Gone, gone, it's gone, all gone

(It's gone)

Isn't it beautiful to imagine everything that you have gone through when you lay them down at the altar of God that all you've been through can be gone? I believe that we only become free when we allow God to cleanse us from all unrighteousness and heal our broken hearts. Jesus says in the Scripture that He came to heal the brokenhearted and set us free in Luke 14:18 (KJV),

The Spirit of the Lord is upon Me, because He hath anointed Me to preach the Gospel to the poor. He hath sent Me to heal the brokenhearted, to preach deliverance to the captives, and recovering of sight to the blind, to set at liberty them that are bruised.

Unforgiveness

I do not know where you are on your journey in this life, I don't know what your pain experiences have been, I don't know who has hurt you and to what degree they have hurt you, but what I do know is God desires to heal you and use your story, your journey for a greater purpose. Sometimes we think that we are no longer useful because of the things we have experienced in our lives when it's quite the opposite because of what you have experienced. God wants you to know that your life matters, and there are people who need to hear your story so that you can help others find freedom and peace within and discover the purpose in which God created them. Unforgiveness can be like a ball of chain wrapped around your ankles, and you drag them around if you're on the ground, and if you walk in the water, you sync to the bottom. You must allow God to break those chains that hold you captive to those paint experiences that cluttering your mind and your heart and keeping you from seeing yourself the way God sees you and would allow for you to elevate your soul to be the very best that God has created you to be. Unforgiveness is the entanglement of a soul; in my heart and my mind that has been twisted by the lies of the enemy, that desire is to keep you from experiencing the freedom that God desires for you to live in. In John 10:10, it says the thief cometh not but to steal, to kill, and destroy, but Jesus says I came that you may have life and have life more abundantly.

God desires to see you live in abundance; that abundance is not just in wealth but in a positive mindset, goodness, serve God and others, let the joy of the Lord be your strength, and have the peace of God that surpasses all understanding be your guide. To live in abundance through strength, boldness, and courage that you can face the day-to-day challenges of this life. That is God's abundance, *The Elevated Soul of Life.*

I can remember as an eighteen-year-old freshman in college at Liberty University; we had a chapel service where I heard what the power of forgiveness could do for us and allow God to fill us. Forgiveness is like emptying the soul and allowing God to refill it with all of His love, kindness, and all of His attributes that allow for you to experience the greatness in Christ. After this chapel service, I felt a leading of the Spirit to write my biological father a letter letting him know that I forgive him for my experience with abuse and neglect. I can remember that day I wrote that letter, I was in tears, and although I did not have a relationship with my dad, the freedom that I experienced in that moment of writing that letter, I will never ever forget. Forgiveness is a powerful thing; I believe it opens the eyes of your heart to be able to see yourself the way God sees you. If we only could get to the place where we see ourselves the way God sees us. For many people, we walk around not feeling loved, not feeling pretty enough, not feeling good enough, and that's just not the way God sees us. The Scripture tells us that we were created in His own image. Genesis 1:27 (NIV) "So God created mankind in his own image, in the image of God he created them; male and female he created them." Scripture also says we were fearfully and wonderfully made. "I will praise thee; for I am fearfully *and* wonderfully made: marvellous *are* thy works; and *that* my soul knoweth right well" (Psalm 139:14, KJV).

Attitude of Forgiveness

Learning to live with an attitude of forgiveness is the key to your doors of freedom and opportunity. I am reminded of our Savior Jesus, who was crucified for being good to everyone, spreading love, healing, and preaching the Gospel. Yet as He hung on the cross, He made one of the most powerful statements; He said, "Father forgive them for they know not what they do" (Luke 23:24, KJV). I would suggest that most of the time, the people that hurt you and the incidents that happened to you, and perhaps, the wrong decisions that you made that you find unable to forgive yourself for; all happened out of the "not knowing what we do" state of mind. I'm not sure many people think of the long-term consequences that they leave in the life of an individual that they hurt. At the moment that people choose to hurt others is probably one of the most selfish things that they choose to do; however, I'm not sure if they realize the long-term effects of pain and agony that they subject on someone's life, that sometimes takes years to recover from. The good news is no matter how long it takes, God is chasing you, longing to forgive you, to love you, to cleanse you, and set you on higher ground. Forgive! Find it in your heart, your mind, and your soul to unravel all that has happened to you and forgive those who have hurt and allow God to use you to do great and mighty things.

One of my favorite characters in the Bible is Joseph. I referred to him in an early chapter as he faced many trials of personal mistreatment, rejection, wrongly accused, and yet found himself being the governor in charge of all of Egypt. You see, no matter what happens to us, God is working a plan on our behalf to put us in a place that we would never have ever imagined. Joseph's brothers threw him in a pit but let him to the place where he became great. But Joseph himself came to a place where he had to forgive. The same brothers that threw him in the pit only to be found by slave traders that took him to Egypt came to Egypt during the famine, and Joseph had to come face-to-face with his brother, who had betrayed him for the first time since he was a young boy. Jacob, Joseph's father, heard that there was corn and green in Egypt, and he told his son, "Why are you sitting around staring at each other? Go to Egypt and buy some corn and green so that we may live and not die." Little did Jacob know nor his sons, their brother, Jacob's lost son, was the governor in Egypt and in charge of distributing the corn and the grain.

Can you imagine the scene in the Scriptures where Joseph was minding his own business, doing what he has done the past months and year, and yet, his brothers who betrayed him was on the threshold of coming face-to-face with Joseph on his terms? The key in life is to understand that love conquers all. I can't help but imagine what would have happened if Joseph chose to throw his brothers in jail? What consequences would Joseph have experienced personally and professionally if he mistreated his brothers the way they mistreated him? One will never know the answer to these questions because Joseph chose to do what was right in the eyes of God. He chose to forgive. The way the Scriptures outlined this fascinating encounter is that Joseph was almost like an interrogator to his brothers because they did not recognize him. He was asking many questions because it's only human to think after someone had betrayed you, the way they betrayed him, why are they really there in Egypt? Joseph perhaps thought, are they there to ruin his life once again? These are the same encounters many of us face from time to time, and we are given the opportunity on occasions to forgive, and we allow those negative thoughts to permeate through our minds that we carry the burden of the pain and hurt longer than God desires.

Do not take another day away from your life to enjoy the freedom and abundance in Christ. Do not let someone else cause you the greatness that is waiting on you. Stop it today and choose to forgive. As the story goes in Genesis 42:6-8 (KJV),

> **Now Joseph was the governor of the land, the person who sold grain to all its people. So, when Joseph's brothers arrived, they bowed down to him with their faces to the ground. As soon as Joseph saw his brothers, he recognized them, but he**

pretended to be a stranger and spoke harshly to them. "Where do you come from?" he asked. "From the land of Canaan," they replied, "to buy food." Although Joseph recognized his brothers, they did not recognize him.

Amazing confrontation! Can you imagine? But something happened to Joseph as he was speaking to his brothers; even though he was skeptical of their appearance, he was quickly reminded of the dream that he had shared with the king. In Genesis 42:9 (NIV), "Then he remembered his dreams about them and said to them, "You are spies! You have come to see where our land is unprotected." Joseph was skeptical but desired the true reason why his brothers were in Egypt. Through Joseph's skepticism, he decided to have the brothers prove the reason why they came to Egypt, so he gave them a charge. The brothers told him of their innocence by explaining, "We come from Canaan of a good man who has twelve sons. The youngest being Benjamin and Joseph being the one that was missing from the twelve." Interesting enough, the brothers never said their father's name; however, they did mention Benjamin, which struck a chord in Joseph. I believe it struck a chord in him because Benjamin was innocent of being a part of the wicked schemes that threw

Joseph in the pit. Joseph loves his little brother Benjamin and longs to see him. Joseph also loves his father and longs to see his father. Joseph accused his brothers of being spies, and so he charged his brothers within an assignment in verse Genesis 42:15-16 (NIV),

And this is how you will be tested: As surely as Pharaoh lives, you will not leave this place unless your youngest brother comes here. Send one of your number to get your brother; the rest of you will be kept in prison, so that your words may be tested to see if you are telling the truth. If you are not, then as surely as Pharaoh lives, you are spies!

I love how the Scriptures outline a recipe for us and how to handle those who have betrayed us. There is nothing wrong with making someone prove that they have good intentions about you or towards you. Forgiveness is not necessarily that someone earns; you can choose to forgive and yet make someone prove that they do not desire to harm you or betray you. And as description reveals, if they are willing to earn a place in your life, then they would be willing to carry out your desire to see them prove they deserve the right to be in your life. No, I do not think laughing out loud you should make someone do something out of the ordinary; Joseph longs to see his brother and his father and simply charged them with something they said the reason why they came to Egypt. When someone tries to re-enter your life, they should be able to say the reason why they desire to be a part of your life. Whatever it is that they say, it must align with godly principles and your principles. Forgiveness is a choice. You can choose to forgive and not re-enter a relationship; however, if you choose to forgive and desire or choose to have a relationship with someone, that makes sure you are right with God and choosing to love them the way God would love them. And Matthew 6:14, 15 (NKJV), "For if you *forgive* men their trespasses, your heavenly Father will also *forgive* you. But if you don't *forgive* men their trespasses, neither will your Father *forgive* your trespasses." We must forgive others in order for God to forgive us. The gates of blessings are open when we choose to forgive. This may seem like a difficult process for you, but the reward is much better than the pain and brokenness you are holding on to.

Sometimes God allows for those who hurt us to have to come face-to-face with us that we may have an opportunity to forgive and show love, and sometimes, like in my situation, I wrote a letter, or in Jesus situation, He was hanging on the cross when he asked God to forgive them. So Joseph's brothers set out to prove they were not spies. In Genesis 42 (NIV): "Send one of your number to get your brother; the rest of you will be kept in prison, so that your words may be tested to see if you are telling the truth. If you are not, then as surely as Pharaoh lives, you are spies!" And he put them all in custody for three days. Joseph was determined to find out the true reason why his brothers came to Egypt—this is such a fascinating story of forgiveness and love. There is more so in Genesis 42:16-17, 19-20, "If you are honest men, let one of your brothers stay here in prison, while the rest of you go and take grain back for your starving households. But you must bring your youngest brother to me, so that your words may be verified and that you may not die." This they proceeded to do.

I love how Joseph is illustrating a process in this story of forgiveness. He first saw his brothers, he was Skeptical and spoke to them roughly, so obviously, he had a little anguish in him. Sometimes we try and make forgiveness easy. It's not easy, but it's a must. I hope we can learn from this lesson and find it within ourselves to forgive because God has so much more for us than we know on the other side of forgiveness. We see in verse 20 Joseph moved to a position of grace and mercy. He allowed the brothers to leave and take food to their families. It's hard not to want other people to suffer because we suffered, but God rewards us when we're able to look beyond someone else's wrongdoing and extend grace and mercy. If we only knew how proud it makes God to see his children live a life of love, grace, and mercy.

Benefits of Forgiveness

Now, I absolutely loved the next part of the story when we see the effects of forgiveness. Sometimes we want justice and to be the judge, but if we would sometimes step back and let God be the judge, we experience freedom like no other. Let us take it a step further; in Genesis 42:21 (NIV), "They said to one another, 'Surely we are being punished because of our brother. We saw how distressed he was when he pleaded with us for his life, but we would not listen; that's why this distress has come on us'"— wowwwww! An amazing thing happens when we allow God to do His work. Joseph showing grace and mercy allowed for the brothers to have a self-reflection on their own and were convicted of their wrongdoing. How good is God? You don't have to tell people to say they're sorry. I know as a parent we teach our children that concept. However, how many times in that moment that the same thing happens a while later. Many of us, like children, say we're sorry just to say we're sorry, but if we truly mean it, it will not just be words saying I'm sorry; it would be a sorrowful spirit that brings conviction and leads to repentance. And repentance means to turn from that act or situation to a positive act or situation. A complete 180 degrees and change of behavior becomes evident.

As a coach for twenty-seven years, whenever I had a situation on my team, I would always bring both players in my office and try and get to the root of the problem, and try and help them see the air of their ways and how it affects not just their teammate but also the whole team and the chemistry of the teams. It stops the flow of positive energy throughout families, teams, and organizations. Committing a wrong act towards someone destroys the potential success of anyone in any group. If we could learn anything from the story about a family needing to be restored, to be healed, it is that the power of forgiveness gives God the opportunity to redeem and restore everyone. If your family, team, or organization, or any group has been destroyed by a wrongful act, I employ you to sit before a mentor, a counselor, a pastor; someone in authority that can help you remedy the problem and find the ultimate solution to bringing healing, forgiveness, and love back into your family. God is a redeeming God and can and will restore you and your families. If only I knew these things while I was growing up, perhaps, it could have changed the course of my life and my siblings' lives along the way. Take this opportunity now that you are aware and be a part of changing your history, your present, and your future.

Do not let this day pass you by without taking the steps to forgive. I got to get to the end of this story; the best is yet to come.

So, the brothers set out for their journey, beginning to point the finger at each other for what wrong they caused Joseph. In Genesis 42:22-23 (NIV), Reuben replied, "Didn't I tell you not to sin against the boy? But you wouldn't listen! Now we must give an accounting for his blood." They did not realize that Joseph could understand them since he was using an interpreter. Oh, my goodness, imagine being there in the room and listening to your betrayers converse about what they did to you. Again, we see another way God uses grace and mercy. At first, the brothers thought of the situation they're going through as the reason they were being held, but it goes a step further, and Rueben explains not only why they are going through what they're going through but also says, "We must give an account for his blood." Meaning not only does a person do you extend grace and mercy to have conviction at some point, they realize they have consequences as well. Many times, when we choose to forgive someone and show grace and mercy, we sometimes think whether or not they will suffer any consequences, instead of knowing through the process of forgiveness, grace, and mercy, God will deal with them. Now that you are free because you choose to forgive and extend grace and mercy, you become free and empty of the bitterness and anguish you have carried for so long, and now your counterpart is having to live it— amazing, amazing, amazing!

In my first book, *They Call Me Coach*, I shared my experience with my absent dad. I didn't write the letter to my dad looking for any response; it was a message I heard that prompted me, and I was obedient to do so. However, what I learned was my dad was hospitalized, rattling cirrhosis of the liver and cancer, and my grandmother told me that the letter I wrote him, he carried around in his wallet. Even to the point where he was dying lying in his bed, the letter sat in his wallet by his bedside. When I learned of this, I wept, and even to this point, writing this chapter, I am weeping. You see, ladies and gentlemen, forgiveness is all about you being free, free to live the life God created for you. Not to be held back by the pain of what someone did to you or whatever may have happened to you. Release the pain and anguish and choose to forgive. I am further along in my life where I wish I had become aware of the pain and neglect I carried around for years. Today I feel free, but it has come at a price. I don't want you to have to pay the price for someone else's bad choice, but also forgive yourself for the bad choices you have made. Forgiveness is about forgiving yourself and others and experience the freedom in Christ, knowing that He loves you, cares for you, and desires to do great things in and through you.

As you could imagine, at that moment Joseph heard his brother, he also wept. In Genesis 42:24 (NIV), "Joseph turned away from them and began to weep, but then came back and spoke to them again. He had Simeon taken from them and bound before their eyes." Joseph was being freed right before his brothers, who had betrayed him. But then Joseph did something only true forgiveness, grace, and mercy would do; Joseph blessed his brothers beyond what they ever could have imagined. When I think of this, I think about how God forgives us and blesses us far greater than we ever could have imagined. When it comes to forgiveness, we ask God to forgive us, and He does, we ask others to forgive us, and we forgive ourselves, and I believe within this process of forgiveness, we are elevated to a place where we can experience our peak performance of our lives. The elevated soul of forgiveness is when God blesses us because we choose to live a life of forgiveness toward others and extend grace and mercy and bless them even though they don't deserve it. That's what God does to us; He forgives us and blesses us even though we don't deserve it. The life of Joseph is an illustration of the power of forgiveness, love, redemption, restoration, grace, mercy, and the blessings of God. This wonderful story ends with the brothers on the journey back to Canaan. They stopped to take a rest and eat and feed the horses, only to look in their sack and find not only greens that they thought they had purchased but found silver as well. In genesis 42:25-26 (NIV), Joseph did something miraculous "Joseph gave orders to fill their bags with grain, to put each man's silver back in his sack, and to give them provisions for their journey. After this was done for them, they loaded their grain on their donkeys and left." By the time the brothers got home to their father, Jacob, they were able to tell the story of this leader in Egypt, who at first spoke harshly to them, accused them of being spies, who held them in prison for three days and ultimately blessed them beyond what they ever did imagine. They also told their father of this great leader, who asked that they bring the youngest son Benjamin back for him to see, and the brothers continued to explain their experience. Jacob began to question his son and their motives; as each of them opened their sack filled with grain and pouches of silver, Jacob began to question whether his son had sold their other brother Simeon into slavery. Do you see how a person who sins against you or anyone else returns even when something positive happens for them? They are questioned because of their character.

I can't tell you how much I continue to reiterate

it's not for you to fix them or to require or request the consequences of what may or need to happen to them to change, but watch God as He allows them to experience what their own sin will do to them. For the brothers, their own dad did not believe them because he reflected on a time where the brothers faked Joseph's death because they did not protect him, and now they tell him that Simeon, their other brother, was held back in Egypt because the ruler in charge wanted to see the youngest brother Benjamin. The Scripture tells us in Numbers 32:23 (NIV), "Be sure your sin will find you out." I believe this is the lesson that the brothers are now learning. It's a lesson we all can learn. In conclusion of this wonderful story provides a tremendous lesson for all of us to learn about the power of forgiveness. Joseph's brothers ultimately bring Benjamin so that Joseph can see him, and again, Joseph does something far beyond human expectation. He had his servants serve the finest meal to his brothers, and when he saw his brother Benjamin he had to run out of the room to a private place and wept again. Joseph was moved in his emotions to know that his brother was alive and well. Joseph revealed himself to his brothers and openly forgave them, and they all shared tears together. Even to the point that the king of Egypt, who shared power with Joseph, heard about the reunion and was pleased. Joseph and the king both put together the finest cards and carriages to go and get Joseph's father and all of his family and bless them with all the goods of Egypt and place them in the land that they can have for their own field with the best things that Egypt had to offer.   There was only one thing left to do, and that was for Joseph to be restored to his father. Keep in mind that when the brothers told the father that Joseph was alive and desired for him to come to Egypt, he once again did not believe them *lol*; that same sin of betrayal or lying followed them. The Scripture tells us we reap what we sow; unfortunately, the brothers had some characteristics of lies and deception, therefore, were not trusted. However, when Jacob learned of the carts and carriages that were sent for him, his spirit was revived, and knowing that only his son Joseph could have provided those things. In conclusion of a wonderful story, Jacob and Joseph reunited in the land called Goshen and embraced each other and description says they cried and wept for a very long time, and Jacob's life was fulfilled, and he said, "Now that I know my son is alive and well I can die." What an awesome story the Scripture gives us about forgiveness, grace and mercy, love, restoration, and the blessings of God.

I don't know your situation. I'm not sure where you are with those who have hurt you, but what I do know is for you to be able to experience the elevated soul of life, you

The Elevated Soul

must come to a place where you are able to forgive. Don't let the puppet master of someone else control your life for the rest of your life; let go and let God forgive them. Move on from seeing yourself the way God sees you, get up from where you are, and start moving toward that which God has for you, and I assure you that God has great and mighty things that He wants to do in and through your life if you would only forgive. If I could encourage you in anything in this life, please forgive, take the blinders off by the pain and suffering of your past, unravel the twist and turns of the brokenness that you have experienced, set yourself free so that God can use you. Choose to forgive, extend grace and mercy, and even blessed those that hurt you. Your story, your life matters. There is a great need for people to know of your deliverance, to know your struggle, to know what you have overcome, forgive them and elevate yourself to a whole new life!

You are more than what you see! Is there someone you need to forgive? Do you need to forgive yourself for the mistakes you have made? God loves you, and like Simba and the prodigal son, He longs for your return. Look to Him to find and discover your true purpose!

250

A Self Proclamation

As we close this chapter of our lives, I would like to encourage you to write a Psalm just for you, have it printed on a nice paper, and frame it. As I was studying the Scriptures and allowing God to speak in and through me in writing this book, I felt God speak to me one day as I was studying the life of David. I was reading Psalm 27, which in many scholar's eyes is a Psalm in which David wrote during one of the most difficult times of his life. He found himself on the run from the king, the armies, and his enemies because of false accusations, envy, bitterness, and his own choices. Many scholars believe David wrote this Psalm before he became king over all of Israel. It gives us a perspective that when we encounter and go through some of life's most difficult challenges, God is still with us, as we endure the threats of the enemy who seeks to destroy our lives and keep us from fulfilling the purpose in which God created for us. No matter where you are in the stage of your life, there are a few verses in Psalm 27 that bring comfort to your heart, your soul, your mind, and your spirit. I challenge you to read Psalm 27 and put yourself in the shoes of David as you reflect on your own life and write your own Psalm to God as a prayer offering for Him to elevate your soul through a similar process in which He elevated David to become king over all of Israel.

God has great things in store for you, no matter what you have gone through or are going through. No matter what choices you have made, no matter what someone else has done to you or has wrongly accused you, God can restore you to a greater life than you are experiencing now. Perhaps you find yourself on the run in your life from things that have hurt you. It does not have to be a king or specific person. There are things that haunt us that come from the enemy of our soul, Satan. We could be on the run from a past hurtful, painful experience—death, divorce, neglect, rejection, physical and sexual abuse, alcoholism, drug addiction, criminal mistakes, depression, failure, or any other setback. Many times, we are on the run from those things and find ourselves in a place of unknown or in a desert place like David was. Sometimes these are the places that God opens life's greatest opportunities for you to thrive and be elevated to a greater life if we do as David did. and cry out to the one who can heal us and deliver us from all our troubles. In a previous Psalm in Psalm 23, perhaps David's most famous Psalm, he declares something we should always remember no matter what we go through. He declares, "Yea, though I walk through the valley of the shadow of death, I will fear no evil: for thou art with me; thy rod and thy staff they comfort me surely goodness and mercy shall follow me all the days of my life: and I will dwell in the house of the Lord forever" (Psalm 23:4, 6, KJV).

The one thing I ask from the Lord, the only thing I seek, is that I may dwell in the house of the Lord all the days of my life, and gaze on the beauty of the Lord, and to seek Him and His temple. For in the day of trouble He will keep me safe in His dwelling; He will hide me in the shelter of His sacred tent and set me upon a high rock, then my head will be exalted above all my enemies who surround me, and His secret tent I will sacrifice with shouts of joy; I will sing and worship the Lord. Hear my voice when I call Lord be merciful to me and answer me. My heart says of you seek His face. Do not hide your face from me, oh Lord, do not turn your servant away in anger; you have been my helper. Do not reject me or forsake me, God my Savior, though my father forsake me, the Lord will receive me. Teach me your way, oh Lord; lead me in a straight path in spite of my oppressors. Do not turn me over to the desires of my flesh and my foes, for false witnesses rise up against me with false, malicious accusations. I remain confident of this: I will see the goodness of the Lord in the land of the living. I will wait for the Lord; I will be strong and take heart and wait for the Lord.

EXERCISING YOUR FAITH

Well, it would not be fitting to title a book *the elevated sole* based on a product that was created to improve areas of training and rehabilitation and not talk about the elevated soul of exercising our faith or perhaps putting our faith in action. Would it surprise you to know the Scriptures relate a lot to athletes' training, competition, and athletics? One of my favorites is "Similarly, anyone who competes as an athlete does not receive the victor's crown except by competing according to the rules" (2 Timothy 2:5, NIV). ☐As a young boy who was soooo in love with sports, I had some hesitation when I became Christian about being all in because I thought it meant I would have to give up my love for sports. I had this preconceived idea that I needed to become a choir boy who was religious. Boy, was I wrong! I quickly discovered through the church youth group that the way we live our lives through faith is a direct reflection of many principles that are outlined in the Scriptures. I was blessed and fortunate to have a youth pastor by the name of Jim Stanka, who used to hold the youth group meeting at his house, and prior to our lesson for the night, Jim provided sports like table tennis, throwing the football, basketball, and shooting pool for us to enjoy. Jim Stanka created an environment where we were able to come over to his house and have a lot of fun in an environment of competition, eating favorite snacks and a time with God where we shared principles from Scriptures that were life-changing for me.

I begin to connect the dots that having fun as a Christian was possible and because my youth group leader Jim Stanka loves sports oftentimes, he related messages to sports figures, which was a life-changing perspective for me. I was so pleased to learn that God cares about athletes as well. I know that may sound funny, but when you grow up in the inner city, and you're not involved in a church, every day was consumed by surviving the day in the life of the inner city, and for me, it was playing all types of sports. Whether it was playing football with my friends, or basketball with my friends, or creating our own baseball game by taking the stick out of the closet and making our own baseball with tape, or using a tennis ball. Somehow someway we were going to play some type of sports. I'm grateful to my former youth pastor, now friend, and mentor Jim Stanka, who shattered the mold of what I thought Christianity was as a newborn believer. The Scriptures tell us that we begin our faith journey as infants needing to sip or drink milk. "As newborn babes desire the sincere milk of the word, that ye may grow thereby" (1 Peter 2:2, KJV). Jim Stanka was someone who provided the milk to help give me a perspective that would grow my faith in understanding Christianity and my faith in God. I believe at the beginning of a journey, as believers, we have to exercise our faith. It's a learning process; it's a training process. A learning and training process involves a daily regimen of growing and exercising your faith through reading the Bible and or other sources that build your faith. It's about getting involved in church activities, whether it be youth groups, adult groups, church service, outreach, missions, or community events. As we grow our muscles and train our muscles in our faith, we make sure we put that faith into action in whatever we do. Scripture tells us to "And whatsoever ye do, do it heartily, as to the Lord, and not unto men; Knowing that of the Lord ye shall receive the reward of the inheritance: for ye serve the Lord Christ" (Colossians 3:23-24, KJV).

Understanding My Faith

Many churches today have lost touch with the community and society because we have built churches around growing the number of attendances instead of reaching those outside the church. I can remember when I first became a Christian the joy and excitement that I felt I wanted my friends and family to feel. Those who knew me thought of me as the preacher boy whenever

they saw me; however, it was not my intent to preach to
them necessarily but certainly to share the joy of the Lord,
which had become my strength. To share my new faith
in the God that I believe changed the course of my life
and gave me a greater purpose, and He could do the same
for them. The most difficult thing for me was how do I
balance my faith in Christ with my new adopted family,
which was a committed, devoted Christian family, and my
biological family, which was not Christian, and not many
if any of my friends back in the city were Christians. This
was not an easy task for me. If you were to ask my adopted
parents, Dave and Lynne Johnson, they would tell you that
I was overzealous for wanting to see my biological mom,
siblings, extended family members, and friends come to
the knowledge and saving grace of Jesus Christ. Lynne and
Dave would tell you once I got my license and was able to
drive their cars every weekend or perhaps even on a school
night, I would run to the inner-city wanting and desiring
so desperately to help my biological family. It was like
whenever God showed me something or I learned a new
lesson, I had to go share it with my friends and family in
the city. To me, I was exercising my faith, but what I did
not realize was exercising our faith is not about physically
helping those we love or even strangers. Often it is a call to
prayer and having faith in God to answer those prayers to

change the hearts of those whom you love and even those you don't know. Our faith muscles are not physical, but in a sense, are spiritual. So, what are we doing to exercise and train our faith spiritually?

What I did not realize was the amount of time, gas, and money I was putting into action instead of putting my faith and God in action. As a young believer, I thought it was my job to change people. God created your loved ones, your friends, and your extended family members, and He has a plan and a purpose for their lives just as He had for you. And yes, you are to use your life in Christ to be a spiritual influence on them that would perhaps lead them to Christ. However, it is not you who will change the heart of man; it is the loving God who created them. I had to shift my focus into understanding that God had a calling on my life, yet this was a difficult process because there was a part of me that was saying I was leaving my family and friends behind. I can remember a conversation with Dave and Lynne Johnson; when I was so tired and weary because I was waking up early to go to school, getting my homework done, going to practice, and sometimes running from Katy, Texas, to Houston to help my family and getting back late. This level of concern and commitment was wearing me out. Dave and Lynne Johnson had to help me understand my newborn faith as it relates to impacting and influencing those we love and those who we come in contact with. Unless they shared with me was about Jesus when spoke to a certain man about his father who died and the man's desire to go to the burial and another man who wanted to say goodbye to His family.

> **And he said unto another, Follow me. But he said, Lord, suffer me first to go and bury my father. Jesus said unto him, Let the dead bury their dead: but go thou and preach the kingdom of God. And another also said, Lord, I will follow thee; but let me first go bid them farewell, which are at home at my house. And Jesus said unto him, No man, having put his hand to the plough, and looking back, is fit for the kingdom of God.**

> **Luke 9:59-62 (KJV)**

I believe this is a principle Jesus was simply sharing that when we choose to follow Him, our family and friends will be taken care of because He says go and preach the kingdom of God. By preaching the kingdom of God, Jesus promises that our loved ones will also inherit the kingdom of God. Dave and Lynne taught me that as I grow and go in God that He will take care of my family and friends. Ladies and gentlemen, I sit before you today and declare the principles of God are true. My biological mother, Gladys Coleman, is a Christian and serves in her church. My sister Stephanie is a Christian and served in her church, my brother Brian is a Christian and became a deacon, my brother Willie is a Christian serving the Lord, my brother Jessie is a Christian, and my brother Johnny is not only a Christian, but he is a pastor, and he pastored a church in our hometown of Bunkie, Louisiana, for over twenty years. God is faithful! Furthermore, my extended family, Jacqueline Coleman, who works with me in my organization, is my big cousin, but more like a big sister. She is a devoted Christian, and all of her family, my best friends who are like my brothers, Freeman family, they are all Christians. Unfortunately, we lost who I call my other mother, Betty Freeman, to cancer, but she was a devout, loving Christian woman, so we will see her in heaven one day. I have one brother, Wallace, whom I am still praying for to come to the saving knowledge of Jesus Christ.

You see, Dave and Lynne Johnson taught me a valuable lesson as a new Christian in the faith. Faith is not what we trust and believe in ourselves to be able to do but, it's putting our faith and hope in Jesus Christ and trusting that He will answer our prayers and honor our efforts in growing the kingdom. Matthew 6:33 (KJV) says, "Seek ye first the kingdom of God and all of his righteousness and all these things shall be added onto you." Oftentimes we are afraid that something will happen that day or tomorrow and operate in that fear, which takes away the faith that we placed in God. We need to exercise our faith in God's promises. Jesus tells us not to worry about tomorrow; in fact, it's in the very next verse in Matthew 6:34 (NIV) "Take therefore no thought for tomorrow: for tomorrow shall take thought for the things of itself. Sufficient unto the day is the evil thereof."

Prioritize and Build Your Faith

As you begin your journey, perhaps as a new believer, grow and exercise your faith by placing more trust in God rather than yourself. Your responsibility is to grow and exercise your faith by being about the Father's business. Jesus Himself struggled with this concept as well while He was young. If you recall, as a boy traveling with His parents, He wandered off and caused his parents to worry. Once He was found, He asked His parents why they were looking for Him? He then gives a powerful response to them "I must be about my Father's business!" Check this story out:

> **After the festival was over, while his parents were returning home, the boy Jesus stayed behind in Jerusalem, but they were unaware of it. Thinking**

he was in their company, they traveled on for a day. Then they began looking for him among their relatives and friends. When they did not find him, they went back to Jerusalem to look for him. After three days they found him in the temple courts, sitting among the teachers, listening to them and asking them questions. Everyone who heard him was amazed at his understanding and his answers. When his parents saw him, they were astonished. His mother said to him, "Son, why have you treated us like this? Your father and I have been anxiously searching for you." "Why were you searching for me?" he asked. "Didn't you know I had to be in my Father's Business?" But they did not understand what he was saying to them.

Luke 2:43-50 (NIV)

Do you find it funny as I do that they went a full day without realizing He was with them on their journey back home? Many theologians think because of His spiritual presence, they thought He was with them before their fresh minds did not see his physical presence. Something very interesting for us to think about. Perhaps when we're going through times where we don't see Him, we can feel His presence. Also, ironically it took them three days before they found Him in the temple courts. Many scholars and theologians believe this was projecting what was to come, that He would be gone for three days in His burial and appear to them again physically in the temple courts. The Word of God can be fascinating and very interesting; you dive into some of the little nuances that the Scripture depicts, trying to illustrate principles and guidelines for us to follow. Also, isn't it interesting that He tells us in verse 50 that His parents did not understand what He was saying? This is such a great principle for us as Christians as we grow in our faith and choose to exercise our faith in living a life that is pleasing to God. Many times, people will not understand the choices you make and the life you live but be of good faith, stay committed to your Father's business. As you begin to grow and exercise your faith, trust, and belief, God will provide for you and bring you through everything you will face. Growing and exercising your faith will have pain involved in the process. It doesn't mean God has forgotten about you and is causing you to suffer. Our faith grows as we conquer challenges along the way and endure some painful experiences, just like in sports. Scripture says, "No temptation has overtaken you except what is common to mankind. And God is faithful; he will not let you be tempted beyond what you can bear. But when you are tempted, he will also provide a way out so that you can endure it" (1 Corinthians10:13, NIV). I remember when I was a young coach, even though it was a new program with a lot of beginners in the game of basketball. I scheduled us up against quality and tough teams because I wanted my team to see and learn what it takes to be the best. Even though I felt I knew my team was inferior to other teams and many parents and administrators questioned why we were playing some of the games that I scheduled, in my mind, I had two objectives, and I believe God has similar objectives for us as we go through difficult times or when we face the giants in our lives. My two objectives were: number one, to help my players see what good basketball players look like and what a good team looks like. Secondly, I wanted them to know if they were ever going to be a champion or be the best; those were the kind of teams they would have to beat.

Do you see it was never my intention to hurt or to horn or to cause one of my players to lose heart or lose confidence or not believe in themselves or the process I was taking them through? It was simply about becoming the very best version of myself individually and as a team. I remember the first year of coaching my varsity boys and girls, we were blown out on so many occasions that there were many tears, a lot of discouragement, and some even quit. However, I told them, "If you are willing to put in the work, and you are willing to pay the price, I will give you everything you need to prepare you and help you become winners." God does the same thing in our lives. He has a purpose and ultimate outcome and objective that He wants to achieve in our lives, and His purpose, while it is unknown to us, we have to trust in Him and trust His process. He gives us the same promise I gave my team. He gives us everything we need to be successful and prosperous on our journey of faith.

> His divine power has given us everything we need for a godly life through our knowledge of him who called us by his own glory and goodness. Through these he has given us his very great and precious promises, so that through them you may participate in the divine nature, having escaped the corruption in the world caused by evil desires. For this very reason, make every effort to add to your faith goodness; and to goodness, knowledge; and to knowledge, self-control; and to self-control, perseverance; and to perseverance, godliness; and to godliness, mutual affection; and to mutual affection, love. For if you possess these qualities in increasing measure, they will keep you from being ineffective and unproductive in your knowledge of our Lord Jesus Christ.

Exercising Your Faith

2 Peter 1 3-8 (NIV)

A testament to a group of young people that began a process being an inferior opponent, in the sports world, we say "they were wet behind the ears," meaning they were too young to be successful. But through a process of hard work, dedication, and commitment to doing the right things unifying ourselves as a team, and embodying all of the principles that it took to be champions, we embraced those things and reached our goal of being the best version of ourselves. "I have seen something else under the sun: The race is not to the swift or the battle to the strong, nor does food come to the wise or wealth to the brilliant or favor to the learned; but time and chance happen to them all" (Ecclesiastes 9:11, NIV). The race that God has us in is like a season of competition; it is not swift. You will win some and lose some. There will be battles that go your way, and some of you may be humiliated. My teams were beaten by fifty, sixty, seventy, eighty, ninety, and I believe we got beat by one hundred points one game—complete disaster! However, in the end, none of those kids remember those times as they are now a joke for laughter. The joy is in knowing they became champions. God is going to take you on a journey where you will face many battles and testing of your faith, but He will be right there with you to help you along the way.

Exercising and training our faith as we mature in the faith is about demonstrating the character of Christ in our lives. Each day we get up and begin with an exercise of perhaps reading, worshiping, serving, and praying to prepare us for each day. As we walk out the doors into living ours lives, we are prepared for challenges that will test our faith. Just as athletes, individuals, and fitness competitors train and exercise their muscles to prepare for a competition or just be in great shape, we must prepare our faith for the performance against your greatest competition. David was prepared for Goliath because while he was a shepherd boy, he watched over the sheep and many times had to fight off lions and bears to protect the sheep. The reason why David was so confident when he faced a giant called Goliath from Philistines was that he had previous victory over lions and bears. Each challenge that you overcome should build your faith and prepare you for the next challenge.

Maturity in the Faith

Mature faith no longer sips and drinks milk; the Scripture describes maturity as one who goes from drinking milk to chomping on the juicy steak. "For everyone that useth milk is unskillful in the word of righteousness: for he is a babe. But strong meat belongeth to them that are of full age, even those who by reason of use have their senses exercised to discern both good and evil" (Hebrews 5:13-14, KJV). The Scriptures tell us their senses are exercised to discern good and evil. The more mature we become, the more capable we should be able to do what is right. Maturity in the faith also brings about bigger trials and challenges. Remember, the more you exercise your faith and prepare for your faith journey, the more God will allow you to be challenged. Same concept as myself in developing and coaching my teams to championships. The more growth you show, the more you will be tested. God has a level of greatness He wants to achieve in your life to affect and grow the kingdom. I believe your greatest trials will come as you seek to discover your purpose. For most, our purpose is not clearly identified, so we spend a lot of time wondering and searching for significance before we walk into our calling or our purpose. It takes great faith to keep moving in the direction of your purpose on your journey, especially when we have no idea the specifics regarding what waits at the end of that journey.

God is always working on our behalf to accomplish a purpose. The key is for us to *keep the faith* during our greatest trials. Exercise and grow your Faith muscles during this time and prepare yourself for the great future God has for you. Hebrews 12:1 (NIV) says, "Therefore, since we are surrounded by such a great cloud of witnesses, let us throw off everything that hinders and the sin that so easily entangles, and let us run with perseverance the race marked out for us." Our journey of faith can be compared to a race, and it will require some perseverance, especially when it looks like times are getting tough.

Imagine the step of faith Peter was faced with. I read a great book by John Ortberg titled *If You want to walk on water, you've got to get out of the Boat.* In this book, John Ortberg describes faith in the form of a step out of the boat. He takes this concept from the story of Peter, who while with the other disciples on a boat, saw what they thought was a ghost, and Jesus spoke and said, "It is I!" Peter then challenged Jesus saying, "Lord if it is you, command me to come to you on the water."

> **Shortly before dawn Jesus went out to them, walking on the lake. When the disciples saw him walking on the lake, they were terrified. "It's a ghost," they said, and cried out in fear. But Jesus immediately said to them: "Take courage! It is I. Don't be afraid." "Lord, if it's you," Peter replied, "tell me to come to you on the water." "Come," he said. Then Peter got down out of the boat, walked on the water and came toward Jesus. But when**

he saw the wind, he was afraid and, beginning to sink, cried out, "Lord, save me!" Immediately Jesus reached out his hand and caught him. "You of little faith," he said, "why did you doubt?"

Matthew14:25-31 (NIV)

There is an outline of events that takes place in this story that can help us when we are being prepared to achieve our greatest feat.

1. Step of Faith: Every great feat you want to accomplish in your life will involve something completely and totally outside of your knowledge, skill, and experience. God wants you to demonstrate the amount of faith beforehand; it will require you to lead the people or perform the necessary tasks. Sometimes this calling will be something you would have never imagined. God desires to show you great and might things because it's going to require faith, "Jesus replied, "Because you have so little faith. Truly I tell you, if you have faith as small as a mustard seed, you can say to this mountain, 'Move from here to there,' and it will move. Nothing will be impossible for you" (Matthew 17:20, NIV).

2. Stay Focused: Many things will serve as a distraction

to get your eyes off God and your purpose. You must not look at the winds of adversity, and the joys and pleasures of this world keep you from staying focus. Trust me; there will be many different things come at you. The enemy of your soul does not want you to discover and live out your purpose.

> **Fixing our eyes on Jesus, the pioneer and perfecter of faith. For the joy set before him he endured the cross, scorning its shame, and sat down at the right hand of the throne of God. Consider him who endured such opposition from sinners, so that you will not grow weary and lose heart.**
>
> **Hebrews 12:2-3 (NIV)**

3. Do Not Be Afraid: I surmise there will be times when a spirit of fear may come on you, rebuke the fear and exercise your faith. Believe in the promises God gave you from the beginning. God will be with you during those times where fear tries to overtake you. Remember exercising your faith requires exercise and training by reading the Word and or books that will encourage you, pray without ceasing, worship in His presence in music and song, and lastly, find a way to serve. Faith over fear! Jesus actually told Peter before he even stepped out of the boat,

"Do not be afraid it is I." When adversity comes, do not be afraid. The same God that called you to the purpose you find yourself walking in is the same God that will save you. "So do not fear, for I am with you; do not be dismayed, for I am your God. I will strengthen you and help you; I will uphold you with my righteous right hand" (Isaiah 41:10, KJV).

4, Cry Out: When you feel like you are sinking, cry out to God. Don't allow bitterness and anger to fill your heart. Send against humble yourself and cry out to God He is an ever-present help in a time of need. Remember, even Jesus cried out to His Father as He endured the cross. "About three in the afternoon Jesus cried out in a loud voice, "Eli, Eli, lama sabachthani?" (which means "My God, my God, why have you forsaken me?") (Matthew 27:46). I know as men we struggle with crying, but I have found in the Christian faith it is necessary to cry out! The very words explain the concept. Whatever is hurting you on the inside, cry it out to God. "Then they cried to the Lord in their trouble, and he saved them from their distress" (Psalm 107:19, NIV).

5. Save Me: The last part of the verse says Jesus reached down and saved Peter. God will not let you drown in your situations. When He pulled Peter up, He said, "Oh

ye of little faith." What is the faith that will save you? Jesus uses this as an example, and in many of the instances He healed people, He told them, "Because of your faith you have been made whole, because of your faith you have been healed." Whenever you find yourself in a situation, you must exercise your faith. It's a small step in the right direction. The truth is He's already saved us. We have been bought with a price and sealed with a victory when He died on the cross. However, in our lives, when we find ourselves facing adversity, we must hold on to our salvation. A great Scripture to remember is "For it is by grace you have been saved, through faith—and this is not from yourselves, it is the gift of God" (Ephesians 2:8, NIV).

His grace and mercy were and always will be extended towards you.

As I studied this story, perhaps what Jesus was illustrating in this one story, simply put, three things. It's going to take a step of faith to begin your journey, as I have been saying. It will take maintaining your faith staying focus on Jesus to go through whatever you have to go through. And it will take faith to accomplish and fulfill the call and purpose in your life—fascinating! God is allowing you to put your faith in action and demonstrate perseverance. When He sees us do that, and believe, and not doubt, we will fulfill the purpose in which God has called us.

> **Because you know that the testing of your faith produces perseverance. Let perseverance finish its work so that you may be mature and complete, not lacking anything. If any of you lacks wisdom, you should ask God, who gives generously to all without finding fault, and it will be given to you. But when you ask, you must believe and not doubt, because the one who doubts is like a wave of the sea, blown and tossed by the wind.**
>
> **James 1:3-6 (NIV)**

Embrace and Enjoy Your Faith Journey

This faith journey is a wonderful journey when you stick close by your provider, protector, your friend in Jesus. When you reach the point in your faith journey, Jesus says, "I no longer consider you as servants; I call you friend." I have a friend in Jesus. The beauty of this Scripture tells us, "One who has unreliable friends soon comes to ruin, but there is a friend who sticks closer than a brother" (Proverbs 18:24, NKJV).

Arise, go to Nineveh, that great city, and cry against

it; for their wickedness is come up before me. But Jonah rose up to flee unto Tarshish from the presence of the LORD, and went down to Joppa; and he found a ship going to Tarshish: so he paid the fare thereof, and went down into it, to go with them unto Tarshish from the presence of the LORD.

Jonah 1:1-3 (NIV)

Jonah knew and felt the presence of God, but when God told him to go to Nineveh, Jonah ran from his call. Many Christians run from their call, not being ready to surrender to God, and it takes a circumstance or even tragedy to get us to surrender. Jonah found himself in a precarious position on a ship that was now faced with a storm. In great fear, the shipmaster was afraid, and each of them was trying to figure out why is God allowing this to happen? Meanwhile, Jonah was down at the bottom asleep. The men on the ship decided to cast lots to see who is responsible for God bringing this upon them. Have you found yourself in situations where you thought to yourself, why is this happening to me? I know I have. Two years ago, I had four car accidents, and after each one, as I laid around in pain and disgust, I thought, *what in the world is happening to me, and why is this happening?* So, the men decide to cast lots, and of course, the lot fell on Jonah. Imagine at that moment, what thoughts and feelings went through Jonah's mind? What I find peculiar is the men asked Jonah who he was and where did he come from. This fascinates me because sometimes, as Christian, we run from or hide the fact that we are Christians in order to be accepted. But when we find ourselves in desperate need of help from others and from God, we then express who we truly are. Jonah responded to the men on the ship and told them he was a Hebrew, a devout believer in God. And because he revealed who he was, the men asked, "why did you bring this upon us"? In this story, because the men knew Jonah was a follower of Christ, they did not throw him overboard immediately; they actually tried to row against the wind. However, they could not, so they threw Jonah overboard.

I love small nuggets that the Bible gives us, little nuggets of wisdom. Here's some insight for you when you find yourself running from your call. 1) God loves you so much He chases after you. He didn't let Jonah run off and forget about him; He actually cared enough to do something to get his attention. Oftentimes many people confuse this kind of love with dislike. God does not dislike you while you're running from your call. He actually cares enough to chase after you—stop running! 2) Even when you are on the run, God will show you favor by actually putting people in your path to help you realize who you are. The fact that Jonah had to confess who he was, gave an opportunity for the men to try and help him. 3) God won't let others save you because He wants to save you, so you'll know He loves you and get your attention so that you look to Him and only Him. Jonah, when all else failed, had to call on God. Sounds familiar, isn't that what Peter had to do when he was sinking? People, I'm trying to tell you God's method is very simple, don't make it complex or confusing that's where the enemy trips us up. Scripture tells us the devil is the author of confusion. "For God is not the author of confusion, but of peace, as in all churches of the saints" (1 Corinthians 14:33, KJV). In conclusion of this story, Jonah is tossed overboard, and Scripture says God sent a fish to swallow him up—what an amazing God!

Once again, an opportunity for harm to come to Jonah God uses a fish to save him. My people, God will go to the ends of the Earth to save you, but at some point, you must wake and realize God is calling you through these circumstances. The Scriptures tell us in Jonah 2:1-4 (KJV),

> Then Jonah prayed unto the LORD his God out of the fish's belly, And said, I cried by reason of mine affliction unto the LORD, and he heard me; out of the belly of hell cried I, and thou heardest my voice. For thou hadst cast me into the deep, in the midst of

the seas; and the floods compassed me about: all thy billows and thy waves passed over me. Then I said, I am cast out of thy sight; yet I will look again toward thy holy temple.

What will it take for God to get your attention? At the end of the day, it was Jonah finally exercising his faith that finally saved him as he cried out to God in repentance. You can stop running, repent, and God will restore you, clean you up and get you back on your way to fulfilling your purpose. Imagine the *clean up* job had to do on Jonah; I mean literally clean him up after being spit out of the mouth of a whale or great fish—ewwww! Lol! No matter how bad your situation, circumstances, and bad choices, God is chasing after you, and He desires to use your brokenness to fulfill a greater purpose. Will you allow Him? Will you step into faith, and exercise your faith, and trust a loving God with your faith journey? One of my favorite gospel songs is by Tasha Cobb-Leonard. She uses the concept of "Gracefully Broken" to demonstrate that God does not want harm to come to us. He desires to break us, set us free, so we may experience His goodness to us, and fulfill the call on our lives. I encourage you to listen to this song, but for now, here's the lyrics.

Gracefully Broken

The Elevated Soul

God will break you to position

He will break you to promote you

And break you to put you in your right place

But when He breaks you (Yeah) He doesn't hurt you,

He doesn't

When He breaks you He doesn't destroy you, He

does it with; grace

Anybody been gracefully broken?

Thank You, Lord, thank You

So Father tonight, we're broken before You

Thank You for handling us with grace (Yeah)

Just lift your worship right there in this moment

Take all I have in these hands

And multiply, God, all that I am

And find my heart on the altar again

Set me on fire, set me on fire (c'mon sing)

Take all I have in these hands

And multiply, God (God), all that I am

And find my heart on the altar again

Set me on fire, set me on fire

Here I am, God

Exercising Your Faith

Arms wide open

Pouring out my life…

I can speak from my knowledge and experience; my faith journey has taken me places I never thought or even dream of. As a kid growing up in the inner city, my friends and I would pretend we were a certain player when we played sports. We got in trouble for spraying paint on our white T-shirts, our favorite players' names and numbers—lol. So much for buying jerseys like kids do today. Even if they were available, we would not have been able to afford them. At that time, we only admired and wished that we could be those players, and we would say, "One day, I'm going to play professionally like him." However, I don't recall ever talking about what college we wanted to attend or how this desire would be accomplished. I look at my life now as I am just about to finish writing this book. What God has done in my life I only could have dreamed of. As I reflect back on the call of my life when I was offered an opportunity to leave home and go out to this Christian school in Katy, Texas, I had no idea where God was taking me. All I knew it appeared to be an opportunity to play basketball for a coach named Dave Stallman, who cared enough to give this strange black kid from inner-city Houston, an opportunity to attend a Basketball Camp in

Clearwater, Florida, of a Hall of Fame Basketball Player's Camp in Pistol Pete Maravich. A life-altering experience that has taken me places unimaginable.

I ask myself, what if I would have declined the offer to camp? What if I would have declined the opportunity to attend a Christian School at Faith West Academy? What if? One will never know. However, what I know is it was the best decision of my life. That decision obviously led me to a lifesaving relationship with Jesus Christ, and He has been my rock, my salvation, and my everything. My life has not gone without many challenges. If you read my first book, *They Call Me Coach,* my life has had many disappointments from finally realizing the physical abuse of my dad, the neglect, and rejection, which planted seeds of doubt, fear, insecurity, and brokenness that I was unaware of until I found myself all alone after my second divorce. As I went through the creation and inventing of The Elevated Sole of the Training and Rehabilitation Boot, I finally realized that led me to many failures, disappointments, and broken relationships. Through it all, I had to exercise my faith and know *my God will not fail me*. Though, there is trouble on every side, *my God!* God has brought me a mighty long way, and there is nothing, absolutely nothing, that could make me regret my faith journey. "The Lord bless you and keep you; the Lord make his face shine on you and be gracious to you; the Lord turn his face toward you and give you peace" (Numbers 6:24-26, NIV). The Lion King "Ah yea, the past can hurt but guess what it's in the past!"

Don't drag your past hurts, pains, insecurities, disappointments, and brokenness into your present or future. God will use all of it to fulfill His purpose in your life. For we know in all things, God will work it together for our good. Paul says in Philippians,

> **But whatever were gains to me I now consider loss for the sake of Christ. What is more, I consider everything a loss because of the surpassing worth of knowing Christ Jesus my Lord, for whose sake I have lost all things. I consider them garbage, that I may gain Christ and be found in him, not having a righteousness of my own that comes from the law, but that which is through faith in Christ—the righteousness that comes from God on the basis of faith.**

> **Philippians 3:7-9 (NIV)**

Everything I have endured has built my faith, and because I know where God found me and where He has brought me, I trust He will continue to take me places I would never have imagined. Say yes to Jesus and start your faith journey, and your faith will be made whole. If you already said yes, get focused and serious about it. Begin to apply the things that will elevate your soul on your faith journey. God has great and mighty things He desires to show you. Stephon Leary, a kid whose mom had the courage to run from an abusive dad in the middle of the night, gave him an opportunity to a life I could only dream of. I'm grateful to say this will be my second book, hopefully, a best-seller. I took Basketball as a player as far as I could go on these knees, lol. I became a successful high school and college coach NCAA Division 1 assistant and head coach at Division 2, a teacher, an athletic director, school counselor, NBA agent/trainer, business owner of Reaching New Heights Basketball and Training Program/Shooting Stars AAU, best-selling author, inventor with a patent, and a motivational speaker. Who would have ever thought? Not me! God will take you places and help you become someone that makes you proud and your parents, friends, and family members proud too. Exercise and train your faith and watch where God takes you. The best is yet to come. To God be the glory forever, and ever Amen!

Good luck on your faith journey; may God bless you!

Love to you all,

ABOUT THE AUTHOR

Stephon Leary, born with first name Stephone, is an inspiring man of God whose life was drastically changed in an instant. As a young man, he took advantage of an opportunity given to him at the age of seventeen by a stranger, a man named coach David Stallman in the summer of 1986. He was blessed with the opportunity to attend the late great Hall of Fame "Pistol" Pete Maravich Basketball Camp in Clearwater, Florida. Stephon Leary was a talented inner-city impoverished kid who had an encounter with coach Stallman at a gym playing pickup ball at Memorial High School in Houston, Texas. Coach Stallman saw something in young Stephon and offered him an opportunity to go attend Pistol Pete Maravich Basketball Camp.

"During that time, being a kid from the inner-city, I did not know who Pistol Pete was. However, once I became aware of just who Pistol Pete was, I immediately became inspired and wanted to impress Pistol Pete."

As a youngster, young Stephon Leary was rough around the edges and was extremely competitive and determined from his growing up in the toughest parts of Houston's

Fifth Ward, Third Ward, South Park, Sunnyside, and Southwest side of town. Young Stephon dominated the camp week, and his team went undefeated and won the Championship. Yet, not to be too impressed with young Stephon's achievements, Pistol Pete asked to have lunch with Stephon on that Friday to close out Camp.

This lunch would be a life-changing conversation for young Stephon Leary. What was supposed to be an exciting opportunity quickly turned into a heartbreaking moment for me. Young Stephon thought this was the best thing that could happen for him being an inner-city impoverished kid who never met a celebrity before.

"However, Pistol Pete gave me some of the toughest news I had heard at that time in my life. He told me, 'While you're the best player here at this Camp, and I think you have great potential to be a great player.' He also told me I reminded him of Nate Tiny Archibald, who was a teammate of his with the Boston Celtics, but he said, 'I give out a Most Outstanding Camper Award to the best camper each week, and I wanted to have lunch with you to let you know I cannot give you that award.' He said, 'your character doesn't fit the award!'"

Stephon was completely devastated and ran out of the cafeteria and cried on a nearby curbside. Coach David Stallman found Stephon and reaffirmed Pistol Pete's words and said, "that's why he invited you to the camp." Coach Stallman saw that same flaw that would keep Stephon from being successful. Coach Stallman also said, "he wanted me to hear Pistol Pete's testimony at the closing of camp."

"As I sat there and heard Pete's testimony, I began to cry." That night at camp on June 18, 1986, young Stephon Leary became a born-again Christian. Stephon now admits those words Pistol Pete shared with him at lunch were the most impactful words he had ever heard. He even has the slogan, *Building Character Through Athletics,* on his team and organization t-shirts. It was almost instantly that Stephon Leary's life changed.

"It was as if God had removed the blinders off my eyes as He did with Paul in the Scriptures."

Young Stephon began to see life from a totally new perspective. Upon returning home, Stephon Leary finally saw the despair and desperation of his situation and wanted better for himself. For whatever reason, Pistol Pete Maravich stayed in touch with young Stephon and became a mentor. Later that same summer, Stephon Leary received a second chance.

"Pistol Pete personally invited me to a Camp in Houston that he was conducting."

Stephon Leary attended, and his character had changed, and he had a better outlook on life as well as treated his teammates and campers well. Stephon dominated the camp, and at the end of the camp, he won every award.

From that point on, God began to open doors Stephon could never have imagined. He began to do inexplicable and miraculous things in Stephon's life. Beginning with meeting another stranger in Lynne Johnson, who Stephon says was like an angel appearing to him. David Stallman had asked Stephon Leary if he was interested in attending a Christian school in Katy, Texas. Upon visiting the Christian school to evaluate whether he would attend, Dave Stallman took young Stephon Leary to a 5:00 a.m. prayer meeting. It was at this prayer meeting that this angel, in the form of Lynne Johnson, encountered young Stephon Leary. Realizing at this moment, Stephon Leary was the only kid at the meeting and the only black person, Lynne Johnson approached him and asked Stephon, "What was he doing at the meeting?" In a shy and startled response, young Stephon Leary said, "I am with him, coach Dave Stallman to visit the school." Lynne Johnson then responded, "How ironic is that?" She further explained and said, "While we were praying, I felt the Spirit of the Lord tell me to offer you a home to live." One can only imagine how amazed young Stephon was when he heard those words. But more importantly, Stephon knew there was a God who loved him and now understood how God loves all people regardless of the color of the skin.

Stephon Leary was born in a small-town Bunkie, Louisiana, where races did not mix, and there were cruel acts of prejudice. Although Stephon Leary played sports throughout his life and encountered other white people, he never felt the kind of love that he felt from Lynne Johnson. Lynne Johnson mentioned that she needed to speak with her husband but invited young Stephon Leary over for dinner. Young Stephon Leary went to the dinner, and once again, God showed up. When young Stephon walked through the door, there were three boys (Jacob, Scott, and Billy and one little girl Jessica). When the young boys laid eyes on Stephon, they noticed he was the guy from the Pistol Pete camp that they had also attended. Stephon also noticed those were the same young boys that he would play around with at the camp. And then there was this little blonde-haired girl named Jessica who runs up to young Stephon Leary, jumps in his arms, kisses him on the cheek, and tells him, "I love you, are you going to be my big brother?" The kind of love and amazement that only God could provide. Stephon also formally met dad, David Johnson, who was also at the prayer meeting but had rushed off to work after the prayer ended. When Stephon Leary returned home, where he lived in the inner-city with his single mother (Gladys Coleman), who was raising seven kids in a two-bedroom apartment, he told his mom that he wanted to leave home to pursue his purpose and a life of success. As you can imagine, Stephon was met with some resistance from his mother, who obviously endured some of the cruelty and racism while in Bunkie, Louisiana. Stephon Leary recalled his mom's response as, "I don't think you should go live with those white people; they might hurt you." However, Stephon tells his mom, "They are not like that mom; they are loving Christian people, and they have treated me with love and kindness and welcome me into their home." With more resistance, his mom was not on board, and yet young Stephon told his mom, "if he was going to be successful, he had to go." His mom finally said, "okay." Stephon left his family to pursue a better life. God opened a door that only God could have! The Johnson family adopted Stephon into their family, Lynne and Dave Johnson, along with siblings (Jacob, Scott, Billy, and Jessica). Stephon had a blindside life story experience that impacted and changed the course of his life forever.

Pistol Pete stayed in touch with Stephon through his senior year and advised me on where he should attend college. With the help of the Johnson family and Pistol Pete, Stephon decided to attend Liberty University and play basketball because of the opportunity to grow as a Christian and discover God's purpose for his life. Stephon was bestowed another honor upon him when Pistol Pete Maravich asked him if he would be a counselor at his basketball camps for the summer of 1987 at Second Baptist (see pic below).

"It was such an honor as I was the youngest among the staff at eighteen years old, and Pistol Pete did not believe in hiring young people. I do not know what Pistol Pete saw in me, but my life was forever changed because he cared enough to have lunch with me that summer in Clearwater, Florida. I'm forever and eternally grateful!"

Stephon Leary spent five years at Liberty as a former college basketball player and a student assistant coach from 1987-1992. After graduating, Stephon spent eleven years as a high school athletic director, teacher, counselor, and coach at Faith West Academy. Ironically Faith West was the Christian school Stephon attended as a high school senior.

Stephon Leary also coached college basketball as division 1 assistant at his *alma mater* Liberty University for four years, helping the Flames go from last in the country to the NCAA Tournament. Stephon served as a head coach at two NCAA Division 2 universities, Palm Beach Atlantic University 05-07 and Texas A & M International University 07-10.

After Coaching in college, Stephon Worked as an NBA agent and trainer with Dutt Sports Services. He is now a business owner of Reaching New Heights Basketball and Training Program and Shooting Stars AAU since 2011. Recently with the shutdown of COVID in 2020, Stephon Leary decided to write a book and became a best-selling author of *They Call Me Coach*. A book outlining and detailing his journey from the time his mother (Gladys Coleman) ran in the middle of the night with seven kids (Willie, Johnny, Stephanie, Wallace, Stephon, Bryan, and Stephanie) from an abusive man and father, and gave Stephon and his siblings an opportunity in life. Stephon Leary shares the many obstacles he broaches and overcomes as God has brought him through. Along this journey between being an agent and a trainer, Stephon Leary also found time to become an inventor and patent holder of the Xxcelerator Training and Rehabilitation Boot. Stephon endured a long, arduous process that challenged him to the depth of his soul. He faced many insecurities during this process, wondering and questioning whether he was good enough and capable of completing this task. With the help of God, and his patent lawyer, Stephon inevitably became an official patented inventor in 2018.

After writing his first book in 2020, Stephon felt lead by God to put aside his Basketball and Training Program and begin to tell his story of love regardless of your race and inspire people; "If I can, you can," which is the slogan of his first book. Stephon decided to become a motivational speaker during the pandemic and has spoken on numerous podcasts and virtual summits. Stephon also has a message of his life's story on an Amazon TV Show called *Speak Up* Season 2. Shortly after speaking and launching his first book in December 2020, Stephon began writing this book, *The Elevated Soul* making it his second book in seven months. Stephon is not sure what God has in store for him next. However, he is a living testament that *you are more than what you see*. His life is an example of what God can do to a life that surrenders to Him.

Stephon wants to inspire others to believe that their best life lies ahead, and sometimes there will be challenges to help you discover your greatest gifts to fulfilling your purpose and becoming successful. Like him, you can overcome whatever situations and obstacles that come your way if you trust in the God you serve and capitalize on the opportunities in front of you. Even if things don't look like what you are used to or familiar with. Sometimes God will use the most unlikely situation to put you in the right position to achieve greatness. Stephon was an inner-city black kid who had no spiritual foundation, no structure, discipline, or educational foundation which was given a chance to make it in this life.

"God has a purpose and a plan for your life. I want to encourage the masses that the bridge of race relations and the power of love can change our perspective and make a difference in this world. God is love, and love is of God. You can make it if you just believe in Him, and "If I can, you can, because you are more than what you see.'"

CPSIA information can be obtained
at www.ICGtesting.com
Printed in the USA
LVHW010106110921
697564LV00012B/548